Tight formation of Spad XIIIs (Courtesy of the National Air and Space Museum, Smithsonian Institution)

SPAD XIII and SPAD VII

The rugged Spad single-seat fighters were among the most well-known weapons of World War I. Their speed and maneuverability as aerial fighters were unsurpassed, and eventually allowed the Allies to establish their air superiority in the war.

Although the Spad was a French plane, it is most often remembered as being the fighter flown by the American ace Eddie Rickenbacker. Rickenbacker's love of the plane was totally unabashed. In his autobiography he described seeing the first three Spads, which were delivered to his squadron on July 5, 1918:

I hurried to the field. There they were, three beauties. They were more impressive by far than any other airplane, any other automobile, any other piece of equipment I had ever seen. This new Spad would mean the difference between life and death. With it, a little luck and continuing aid from above, perhaps I could attain fame in the skies and join the great aces of the War—Lufbery, René Fonck, Billy Bishop, the Canadian, even the great Red Baron himself, Manfred von Richthofen.

One of the Spad XIIIs, which Rickenbacker saw that day, had a numeral "1" on its side. He wanted that plane:

"This is one of the planes for the 94th Squadron, isn't it?" I asked a mechanic.
"Yes, sir," he said. "She's ready to go."
"Well, I'm with the 94th Squadron," I said.
That was all it took. I had it gassed up, strapped myself in and took off. I could have been court-martialed, but I knew I had done right; that wonderful little machine told me so. I headed straight for Touquin, leaving my bag in Paris. I had a Spad.

The first model of the Spad to gain fame was the Spad VII, single-seat fighting scout biplane with a 150 horsepower Hispano-Suiza, 8Aa V-8 water-cooled engine. First flown in April 1916, it was delivered into service on September 2, 1916. Heavier and faster than its contemporary, the Nieuport, the sturdy Spad was a great relief to the French escadrilles, who had had to contend with the poorly designed wings of the Nieuport, which often shed fabric and flew off under stress. About six thousand Spad VIIs were built. Almost every Allied air service, including Rickenbacker's "Hat-in-the-Ring Squadron," the 94th Aero Pursuit Squadron, used them.

The most famous Spad, however, and the model in which Rickenbacker scored most of his twenty-six victories, was the Spad XIII. A single-seat fighter with a 200 horsepower Hispano-Suiza engine, it was an improved version of the VII with more power and two synchronized Vickers machine guns. The Spad XIII was fast, strong, and reliable, and although many planes could outclimb it, few could outdive it. First flown on April 4, 1917, the Spad XIII was placed in service by late May of the same year. At least 8,472 XIIIs were built by the time production ceased in 1919. Eighty-one French escadrille fighter squadrons used the plane. It was the "mount" of almost all the French aces including Charles Nungesser, George Guynemer, and René Fonck, who notched the majority of his seventy-five victories in a Spad XIII. Sixteen pursuit

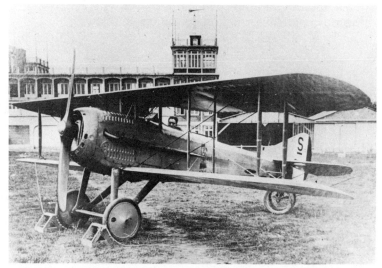

Early Spad XIII in Royal Flying Corps colors (Note wheel chocks and maneuvering dolly) (NASM)

1

squadrons of the American Expeditionary Force in France as well as the British, Italians, and Belgians flew the plane.

The Spads were built in the factories of an ex-silk merchant, Armand Deperdussin. The designs for the planes were the work of the engineer Louis Béchereau, an employee of Deperdussin who had designed the sleek Deperdussin monoplanes that had won both the Gordon Bennett and Schneider Trophy Races in 1913. In 1914 the Deperdussin company went bankrupt. Louis Blériot, a rival manufacturer, was put in charge of the company. He changed the firm's name from Société pour les Appareils Deperdussin to Société pour l'Aviation et ses Dérivés, retaining the S.P.A.D. initials.

By 1915 Béchereau, who had stayed on under Blériot, was looking for a stationary engine to replace the rotary aero engine used at that time. He found it in the new 140 horsepower water-cooled Hispano-Suiza 8A engine designed by Swiss engineer Mark Birkigt. Using both Birkigt's engine and the gun-synchronizing mechanism he designed for it, Béchereau designed first the Spad V and then the firm's first real winner, the Spad VII. Various sizes of Hisso engines and forms of the Spad evolved into the Spad XIII. The prototype Spad XIII (probably S.392) was first flown on April 4, 1917, by Sous-Lieutenant René Dorme.

The plane was constructed out of wood with fabric covering the fuselage. The wings were wire-braced with ribs of spruce-capped plywood. The trailing edges were also wire. They were pulled into curves by tightening the doped fabric, which created their famous scalloped look. The "dope," which was used to treat the fabric, was a highly combustible fluid that drew up the cloth to stretch it tight.

Spad XIIIs had been issued to the *escadrilles de chasse* as early as May 1917. By the fall of that year, the French fighter squadrons were abandoning their Nieuports in favor of the Spads. However, it soon became apparent that there were problems with the 200 horsepower Hispano-Suiza engine. In early 1918 it was reported that mechanical problems with two-thirds of the Spad XIIIs made them unserviceable. Few spare parts for the engines existed. By March 1918, improvements had been made on the engines, including better-quality reduction gears. A more highly compressed 220 horsepower Hispano-Suiza 8Be and later a 235 horsepower 8BEc engine were used which improved the plane's performance. Soon the parent S.P.A.D. company was producing eleven new, improved Spad XIIIs per day.

Since the pilot of the Spad XIII had to handle the plane every moment it was in the air, it was not an easy plane to fly. Lighter, more stable planes were often permitted to "fly themselves." However, the Spad could survive great abuse in the air and rough, bouncy landings as well. A breakdown of some general information on the plane follows:

General Data

Wingspan	26 feet, 5 inches
Length	20 feet, 8 inches
Height	7 feet, 8½ inches
Maximum speed	138 mph
Climb	12 minutes, 10 seconds to 13,124 feet
Service ceiling	21,800 feet
Endurance	2 hours

By early 1918 the modified Spad XIIIs were available. In March, deliveries of the blunt-winged, 220 horsepower or 235 horsepower planes were made for the first time to the United States Air Services. The American squadrons were particularly fond of the plane, buying a total of 893 of them.

Prior to the United States' entry into the war, the only way Americans could serve was with the French Foreign Legion. Since the legion required no oath of allegiance to France, Americans could serve in it without losing their United States citizenship. Several of these American "soldiers of fortune" went on to become members of the Escadrille Americaine, later known as the Lafayette Escadrille, or Flying Squadron. Organized in the spring of 1916, the famed American volunteer unit was named after the Marquis de Lafayette, the French nobleman who fought under General George Washington in the American Revolution. The members of the Lafayette Escadrille loved to fly and were eager to fight. Most of them considered fighting for France the same as fighting for America. During the twenty months that they flew as a unit, the thirty-eight men who belonged to the Escadrille shot down fifty-seven German planes. The adventures of these gallant young Americans provided the folks back home with tales of skill, courage, and self-sacrifice that helped pave the way for America's entry into the war.

Early Spad VII A8798 (Rear of plane is elevated to sight in machine gun) (NASM

Spad VII in Royal Flying Corps colors (NASM)

Early Spad XIII with no squadron insignia (NASM

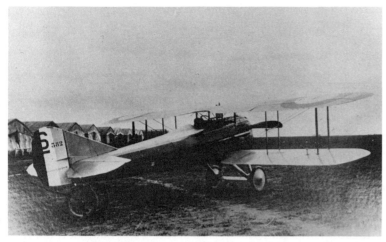

Spad VII (Note maneuvering dolly and canvas-fronted hangars) (NASM)

Experimental Spad with reduction gear engine and swept-back upper wing (NASM)

When the United States did enter the war and the Lafayette Escadrille became part of the 103rd Aero Squadron of the United States Air Service in February 1918, only three of the original seven members were still alive. Many survivors of the Lafayette Escadrille became instructors, flight leaders, and squadron commanders. Men such as Major Raoul Lufbery, the leading ace of the Escadrille, brought a great deal of combat experience to an otherwise inexperienced crew when he became flight leader of the 94th Aero Pursuit Squadron. The 94th, or the "Hat-in-the-Ring Squadron," was the first squadron made up entirely of American pilots and the first American Expeditionary Force unit into battle on April 3, 1918.

The most famous member of the 94th Squadron was Edward V. Rickenbacker. He was born to a German immigrant family in Columbus, Ohio, in 1890. His father died when he was thirteen. Rickenbacker quit school and, in order to help support his family, went to work at a series of factory jobs. It was as an apprentice in the machine shop of the Pennsylvania Railroad that Rickenbacker first discovered what he considered to be an affinity between art and machines. He soon realized that what he really wanted to do was become part of the growing automobile industry. Beginning in an automobile repair garage, he became a race-car mechanic at the age of sixteen, and before he was twenty, a winning driver known by some sportswriters as the "Big Teuton." One story about him in a Los Angeles newspaper said that he was a baron, the disinherited son of a Prussian nobleman who was trying to prove to his father that he could make it on his own.

At first, these types of stories were amusing. However, it was this type of publicity coupled with the fact that his family had retained the old-country spelling of their name—Rickenbacher—that led Scotland Yard agents to suspect Rickenbacker of being a German spy. When he visited England late in 1916, he was detained and stripped of his clothing, which was thoroughly searched for messages. Over a year later, when writing a letter to a friend from a hospital on the Western Front in France, Rickenbacker impulsively signed his name with a "k" instead of an "h" and put brackets around it. His friend back in the States showed the letter to a newspaper and headlines soon proclaimed that "Eddie Rickenbacker had taken the Hun out of his name." From then on, he was practically forced to spell his name with a "k."

While he was in England, Rickenbacker became familiar with the aircraft of the Royal Air Force and with some of their pilots. He wanted to join the Englishmen in fighting the air war over France. Instead, he returned to the United States and arranged to go on a speaking tour to try to convince Americans that the U.S. should join the Allies in the fight. He also tried to persuade the U.S. Army to form a special fighter squadron of racing drivers, "the Aero Reserves of America," but

they said no. Rickenbacker recalled in his autobiography that he was told that it would be unwise "for a pilot to have any knowledge of engines and mechanics." Furthermore, applicants for flight training had to be under twenty-five years of age and a college education or the equivalent was preferred.

When he had a chance to join a secret troop movement sailing to France as a staff driver in May 1917, Rickenbacker grabbed it. He sailed as a sergeant in the U.S. Army with the American Expeditionary Force under General John J. Pershing. When they landed in France on June 26, General Pershing proclaimed, "Lafayette, we are here." Contrary to accounts in the press, Rickenbacker was not a driver for General Pershing. Instead, he often drove for the great air pioneer Colonel William "Billy" Mitchell. It was Mitchell who helped get Rickenbacker into the French flying school at Tours. After earning his wings in just seventeen days, he joined a new unit that had just been formed—the 94th Squadron.

Sent to an aerodrome near Villeneuve, about fifteen miles behind the front line in France, the 94th was assigned a disappointing bunch of cast-off Nieuports to fly. Even worse, the planes had no guns. Therefore, the squadron spent their first days discussing every possible maneuver and every type of attack with their commanding officer, one of the greatest American pilots of the war, Major Lufbery. Rickenbacker had already gained the reputation of only having to listen to an engine to tell what was wrong with it. He was also about the most unpopular man in the squadron in those early days. Reed Chambers, a future squadron member, recalled, "He was big, older, tough as nails. His racetrack vernacular, his profane vocabulary, didn't set right with 'the cream of American colleges.' " However, Rickenbacker was one of the two pilots chosen by Lufbery for the first patrol.

On April 10, 1918, the 94th Squadron flew their Nieuports to an old aerodrome east of Toul. At that time the squadron was commanded by Major John Huffer, who had been born in France and had never been to America. The pilots spent the first day in Toul painting their machines red, white, and blue, and adding their own individual markings. It was Major Huffer who suggested Uncle Sam's Stovepipe Hat with the stars and stripes for a hatband. Lieutenant Walters, the post surgeon, dubbed the group the "Hat-in-the-Ring Squadron." America's first fighting squadron was launched from the aerodrome at Toul and in the next thirty days Rickenbacker scored his first five victories, becoming an ace and receiving the French Croix de Guerre.

Even though he often flew with a stove lid under his seat to warm him, Rickenbacker suffered from a recurrent fever and ear infection. When he was hospitalized during June 1918, he had the time to review his experiences and tactics as a pilot.

Rickenbacker notched the majority of his twenty-two

victories (plus four balloons for a total of twenty-six) in the Spad. Rickenbacker's flights in the plane were sometimes exasperating. Still suffering from an earache and itching for a kill, he went out on a particularly miserable patrol:

I was leading a flight of six Spads over the enemy lines when I saw an aerial free-for-all in the distance. One group of planes skedaddled away from the fight, and seven planes continued on toward us. They were Fokkers.

I was long overdue for a fight. Seven eager pilots from the 94th in seven new Spads were surely more than a match for the seven Fokkers. They saw us. Four turned off, and the other three kept coming. Three hundred yards from us, the three turned and, noses down, throttles wide open, headed for their lines.

It was obvious that the three planes were the bait. My flight was supposed to follow them down, whereupon the four Fokkers would come in on our tails. We did follow them but maintained our altitude. They outran us into Germany. Then I turned in the direction of the other four planes, climbing to about eighteen thousand feet. Sure enough, there came the four German planes back along the lines, looking for us far below. They were either so busy looking below that they did not see us, or they thought we were friendly planes. At any rate, they stupidly flew right at us.

I picked the flight leader. I had him right in my sights. We were only fifty yards apart when he put his ship into a dive. I was waiting for just that maneuver, and I nosed over. It was a target I could not possibly miss. I pushed the trigger on both guns. They both jammed. The flight leader escaped without a scratch.

It was what Lufbery had warned me against, why he had preferred to play the lone wolf. I could not shoot down a German if he was ten feet in front of me. But I was the leader, and if I pulled out of the fight it would confuse my fellow pilots. I made my choice, and I stayed in the fight.

It was a twisting, turning melee. Frequently I could have shot a Heinie down if I had had guns. A couple of times the Germans nearly got me. Two of our pilots dropped out with gun or engine trouble and headed for home. We had

all dropped to three thousand feet and were well inside the German lines. I saw two more flights of German planes racing up, and I called off my fighters and led them home.

I was furious. I had nearly been killed. Even worse, I had not killed any Germans, although they had been right there in front of me. And the whole right side of my head was one blinding mass of pain.

Rickenbacker and his gun sergeant solved part of the gun problem that lay in the ammunition by making a template calibrated to the exact size of a shell case. Each shell was tested and if faulty was discarded. Since the lubricating oil used on the sliding parts of the gun mechanism often became heavy in the low temperatures at high altitudes, Rickenbacker spent much of his spare time honing gun parts. If the gun still jammed while in flight, he hit it with a copperheaded hammer fastened to his right wrist with a leather thong.

After spending another couple of weeks convalescing from more ear surgery, Rickenbacker was again back in the air, involved in the first combined air-and-ground assault in the history of the war. As planned by Billy Mitchell during early September 1918, seven hundred Allied fighters, four hundred bombers, and four hundred observation planes were to support five hundred thousand troops in an assault on the German salient at Saint-Mihiel. The mission of these planes was to contain all German planes within their own lines; to protect Allied supply lines; and to cut off the Germans' rear from the air. During the successful campaign Rickenbacker scored his sixth and seventh victories in a Spad XIII and also had a brush with the dreaded "Flying Circus," the famous squadron of Manfred von Richthofen. Even though the "Red Baron" himself was dead, the pilots of the circus maintained their reputation while flying their Fokker D VII's. As Rickenbacker recalled:

And they outnumbered me three to one. Within two minutes, I recognized them as the finest fliers I had ever faced. I did some fancy flying too, from sheer fright. The four of us whipped our ships around through the air for several minutes. They wanted to shoot me down; I wanted to get

Pilot and gunner in cold weather gear in front of a two-seater Spad XVI (NASM

away. Suddenly an opportunity appeared beneath me. I turned my nose straight down and pulled the throttle wide open. It was for just such a moment that my mechanics and I had babied this engine, and now it delivered. We quickly pulled away. I hurried home to announce my first victory over this elite squadron and my escape.

By September 24, 1918, Rickenbacker had been named commander of the Hat-in-the-Ring Squadron. The 94th had slipped to second place in victories — it was six kills behind the 27th Squadron.

According to Reed Chambers, one of the few remaining members of the original squadron, Rickenbacker had matured: "When he stopped trying to win the war all by himself, he developed into the most natural leader I ever saw."

On the morning of his first full day as commander of the 94th, Rickenbacker set out in his Spad XIII on a one-man mission over the lines. He quickly spotted two LVG two-seater photographic planes protected by five Fokkers, all heading toward the Allied lines. Flying in the glare of the sun he dived on the last Fokker and got him. Instead of attacking Rickenbacker, the other four Fokkers fell off, leaving the photographic planes vulnerable. They had obviously been in combat before because they held their own against his attack:

The two-seaters were only fifty feet apart, and I was directly above them. I sideslipped my Spad to the right. One plane shielded me from the other. I leveled out, kicked my nose around to the left and began firing. The nearest LVG sailed right on through my bullets. It burst into flames and tumbled like a great blazing torch to earth, leaving a streamer of black smoke against the blue sky.

That single-handed double victory won Rickenbacker the nation's highest military honor, the Congressional Medal of Honor.

As an outstanding leader and aerial tactician, he led the 94th Squadron in more victories in the Allied offensive in the Argonne Forest that began the next day. In one morning they shot down two Fokkers and two balloons, helping to pull the 94th well ahead of the 27th. They maintained their lead through their last victory on November 10, ending the war with more Boche victories (sixty-nine German planes) than any other U.S. unit. Rickenbacker himself was the undisputed "American Ace of Aces."

On the night of November 10, 1918, Rickenbacker received by telephone the news that the war would end the following morning. Since their mission was finished at that moment, the war had ended for the 94th and they spent the night in wild celebration, blasting the sky with pistols, machine guns, shells, and rockets. They lit bonfires from barrels of gasoline and emptied every bottle of liquor into a huge kettle to drink from coffee cups.

On the morning of the eleventh, a muggy, foggy day, their orders were to stay on the ground. However, at about ten o'clock Rickenbacker stole off alone, flying one last time over no man's land. He could see both Americans and Germans in the trenches, and was even fired at by the Germans. In his autobiography, he described "the eleventh hour of the eleventh day of the eleventh month":

I was the only audience for the greatest show ever presented. On both sides of no man's land the trenches erupted. Brown-uniformed men poured out of the American trenches, gray-green uniforms out of the German. From my observer's seat overhead, I watched them throw their helmets in the air, discard their guns, wave their hands. Then all up and down the front, the two groups of men began edging toward each other across no man's land. Seconds before they had been willing to shoot each other; now they came forward. Hesitantly at first, then more quickly, each group approached the other.

Suddenly gray uniforms mixed with brown. I could see them hugging each other, dancing, jumping. Americans were passing out cigarettes and chocolate. I flew up to the French sector. There it was not only hugging each other but kissing each other on both cheeks as well.

Star shells, rockets and flares began to go up, and I turned my ship toward the field. The war was over.

NOTE: A surviving Spad XIII still covered with its original fabric is displayed at the Silver Hill Museum, Silver Hill, Maryland, a twenty-four-building complex of preservation, restoration, and storage facilities for the National Air and Space Museum, which is open to the public.

The National Air and Space Museum in Washington, D.C., also has a Spad VII, bearing the Indian-head insignia of the Lafayette Escadrille N. 124, on display.

Captain Edward V. Rickenbacker (NASM)

General Paper Model Construction

In order to construct the model from the pages of this book, you will need a few tools. A No. 11 X-Acto knife works best for cutting out the parts. Try to cut as close as possible to the inside of the heavy black lines. Special cuts, when required, will be explained in the step-by-step instructions. Light pressure with the X-Acto knife can be used for scoring folds, but this requires practice as too much pressure can result in weak folds or cutting through. If you do cut through, a small piece of tape on the back side of the score will repair it. A safer way to score is to use the point of a large needle. Some scoring must be done from the back side of the paper. In order to tell which side to score, follow this code:

– – – – Score on the front and fold the piece away from you.

– · – · – · – Cut short strokes outside the piece, turn over, use the cut marks to line up the straight edge and score. Then turn the paper over. Cut out the part and fold the piece toward you.

A plastic triangle or other straightedge is good for cutting and scoring. White glue is the best for gluing paper and round wooden toothpicks make the best applicators. With a little practice, you will be able to spread a thin film of glue on tabs. Too little glue causes a weak joint; too much glue can cause warping and wrinkling.

Other useful items are small scissors for cutting and trimming; masking tape for holding parts for alignment; a "T" pin for mounting propeller so that it will spin; a drafting compass with a cutting blade would be useful for cutting circular discs for wheels and for small discs when needed; heavy black thread for control wires and rigging; and a selection of markers in colors to be specified for finishing certain areas.

Two versions of the Spad can be built from this book: the Spad XIII serial number 4523 was the Hat-in-the-Ring Squadron's plane with the numeral "1" that Eddie Rickenbacker flew while commanding the 94th Aero Pursuit Squadron; the Spad VII serial number 3198 represents a plane flown by the Lafayette Escadrille. A similar plane can be seen on display at the National Air and Space Museum in Washington, D.C.

The assembly procedure is essentially identical for both planes.

Cut out, score, and fold pilot seat (1). Glue together as shown. (Color seat cushion brown.)

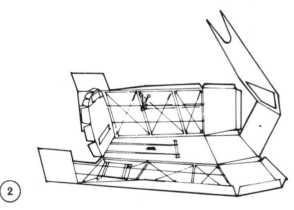

Cut out, fold, and glue together control stick (3) as shown.

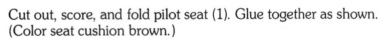

Cut out, score, and fold cockpit interior (2). Pierce hole in center of front bulkhead where shown. Cut out small rectangle in floor for control stick.

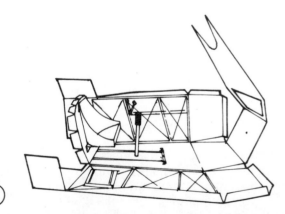

Glue seat and control stick in position as shown.

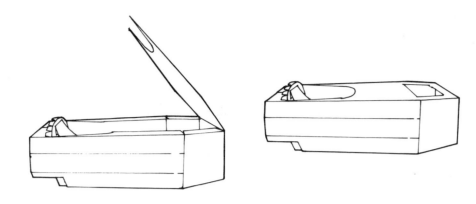

(5) Glue cockpit interior together as shown. (Color top panel light brown.)

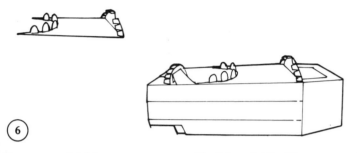

(6) Cut out and fold instrument panel bulkhead (4). Glue in position as shown.

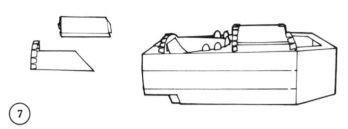

(7) Cut out and fold secondary bulkhead (5) and support (6). Glue in position as shown.

(8) Cut out and fold front cowling ring (7) and radiator shutter panel (8). Glue together as shown.

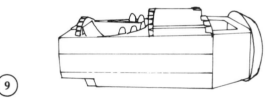

(9) Glue front cowling assembly to front of fuselage. Be sure to line up center holes and to keep shutter lines parallel to sides.

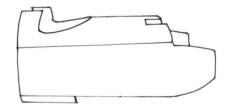

(10) Cut out and fold cockpit outer skin (9). Cut and fold machine gun location slots. For the Spad VII there is one slot. For the Spad XIII there are two.

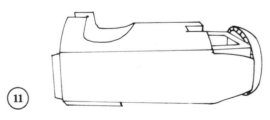

(11) Glue outer skin to interior bulkhead assembly as shown, starting with the top bulkhead flaps. When dry, glue sides in place along lower edges. When dry, glue front edges to sides of cowling ring and hold to curve. Do not glue rear top flaps at this time.

(12) Cut out and glue together 10 propeller hub discs (10). Cut out propeller front (11) and glue onto discs as shown. Burnish down trailing edges as shown. (Color propeller front light brown.)

(13) Cut out propeller fillers (12) and glue to inside of leading edges as shown.

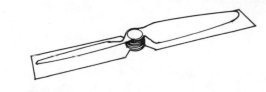

(14) Cut out propeller rear (13) and glue to rest of assembly as shown. (Color light brown.)

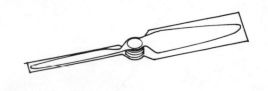

(15) Burnish leading edges up as shown.

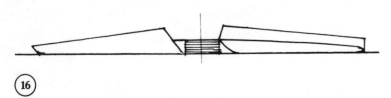

(16) Glue trailing edges, holding flat to table. When dry, apply glue to leading edges and hold in place. When dry, trim back to match front.

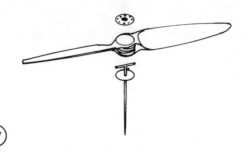

(17) Cut out rear propeller disc (14) and front propeller disc (15). Pass a "T" pin through the rear disc and glue to propeller as shown. Glue front disc in place.

(18) Cut out 12 propeller spacers (16) and pierce centers. Glue together to front of shutter panel, being sure to line up holes.

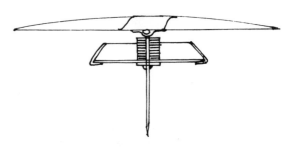

(19) Pass "T" pin shaft through spacers and into fuselage. Cut out and pierce propeller retainer (17). Press over end of "T" pin inside fuselage and apply a small amount of glue around pin.

(20) Cut out and curve secondary cowling strip (18).

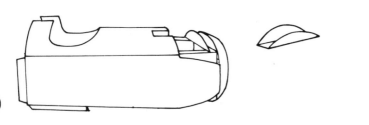

(21) Cut out and fold front bulkhead (19). Glue in place as shown.

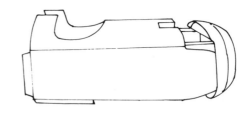

(22) Glue secondary cowling in place as shown, starting with center-line marks and working over each side. Overlap and glue bottom flaps.

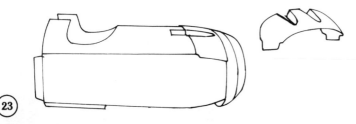

(23) Cut out and form front top panel (20). Cut out and fold machine gun location slots. For the Spad VII there is one slot. For the Spad XIII there are two. Glue in place along front and rear edges as shown. Tuck flaps into sides.

(24) Cut out, roll, and glue machine-gun barrel(s) (21) and machine-gun front(s) (22). Glue fronts to barrels and glue guns to recesses in nose of plane. Insert extended sections under back edges of recesses as shown. Cut 2 sections of round toothpick to match diagram. Color black and glue to fronts of guns as shown.

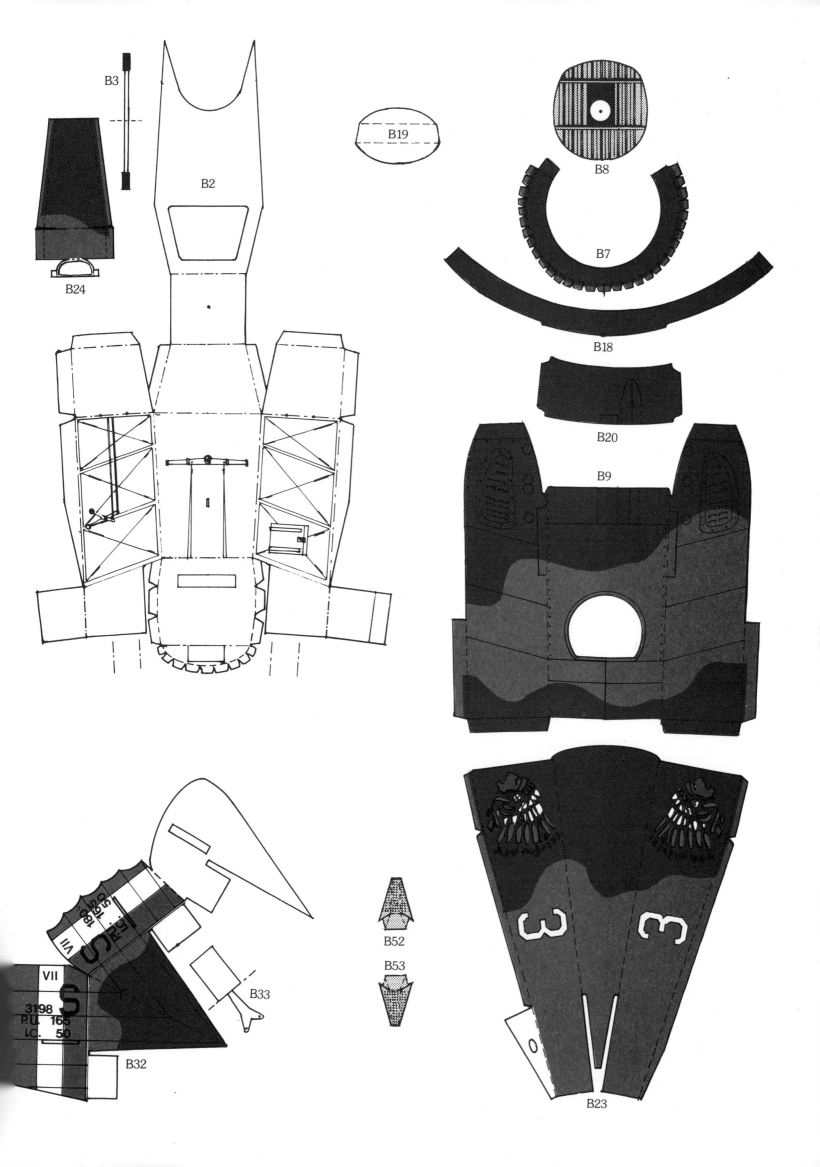

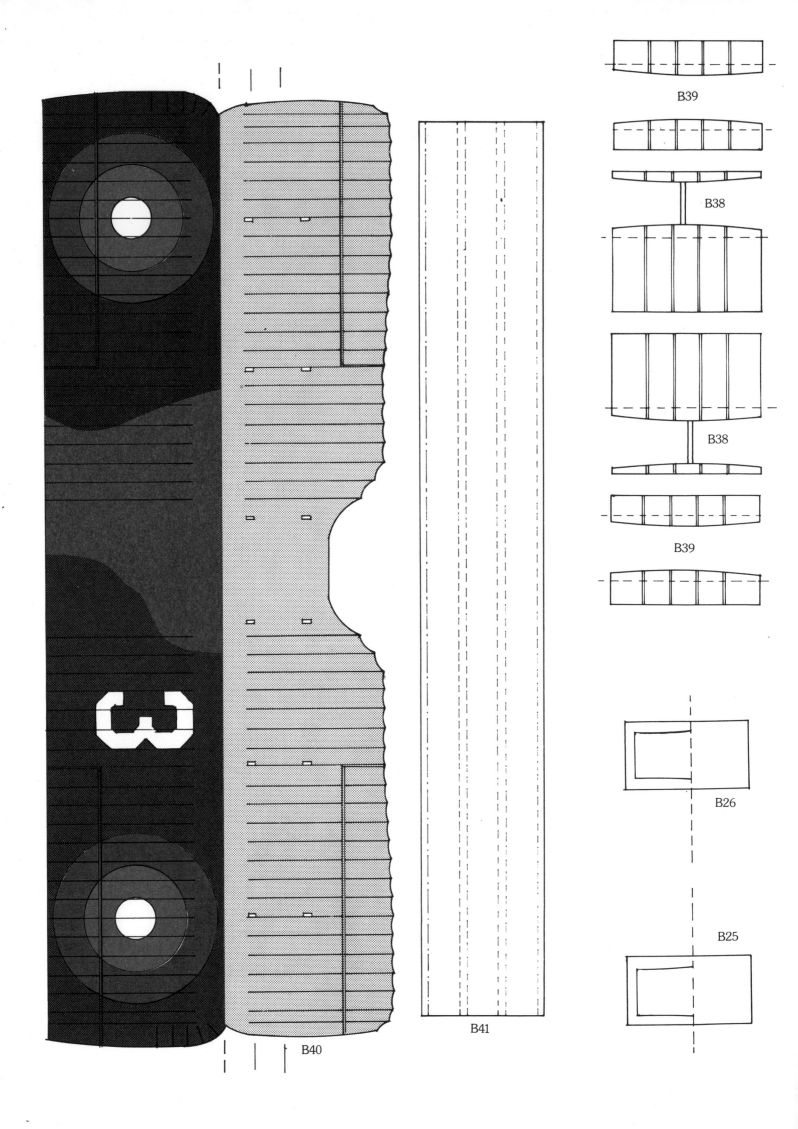

B39

B38

B38

B39

B26

B25

B40

B41

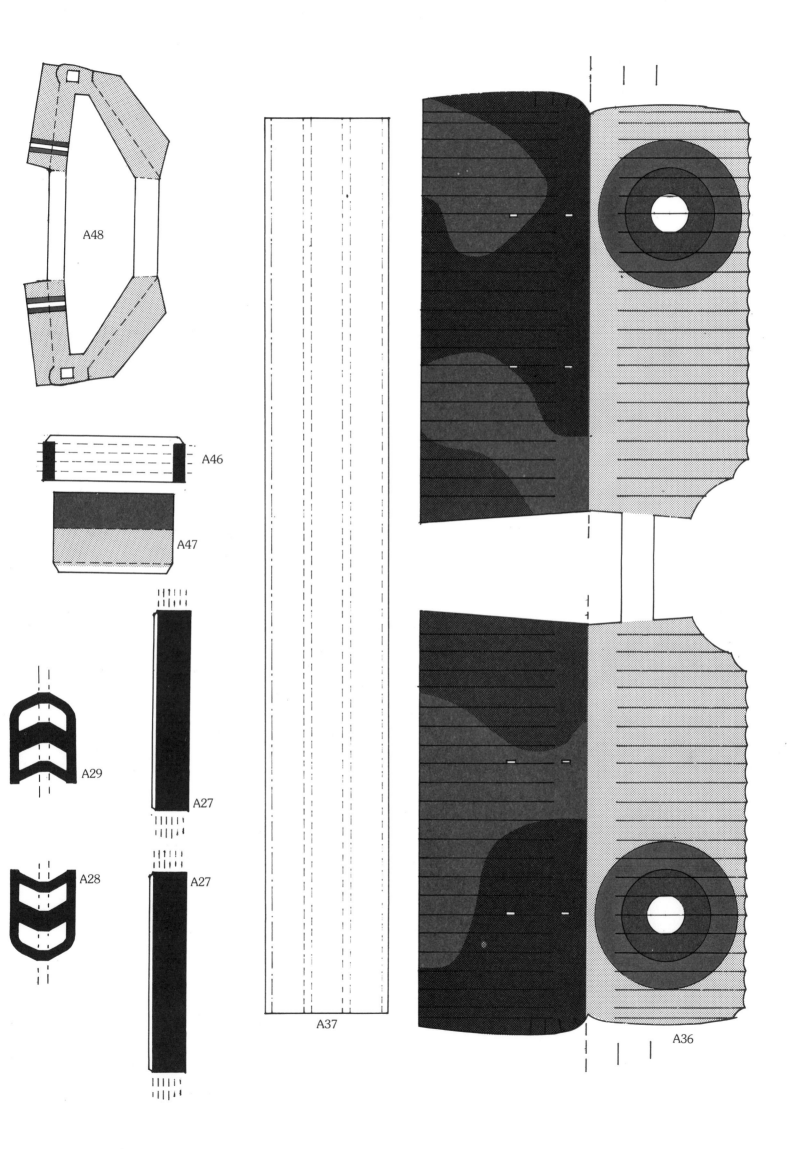

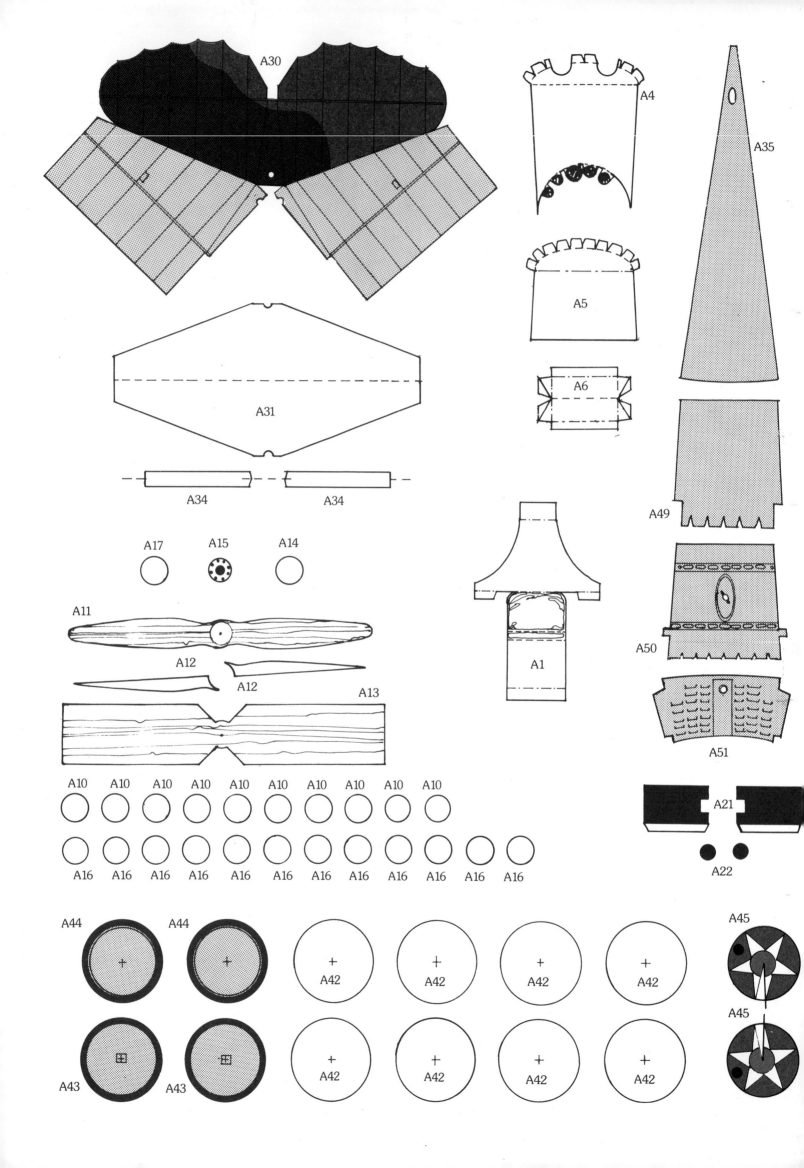

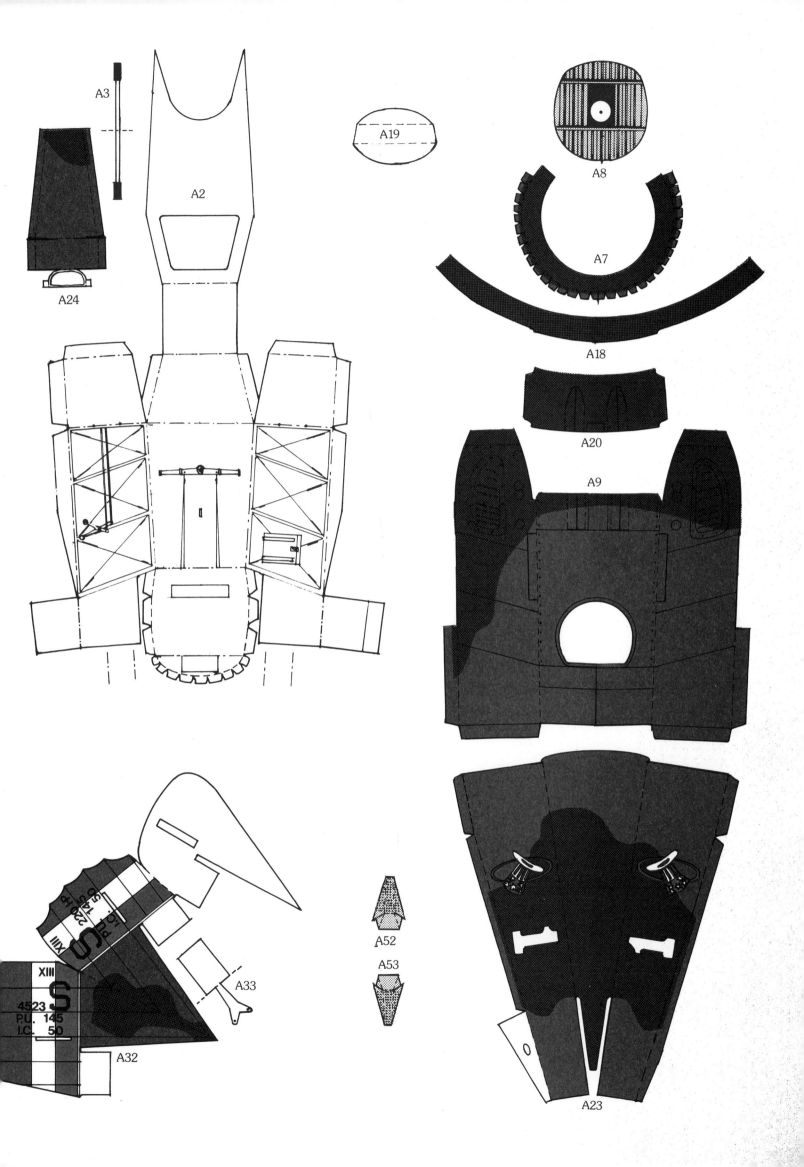

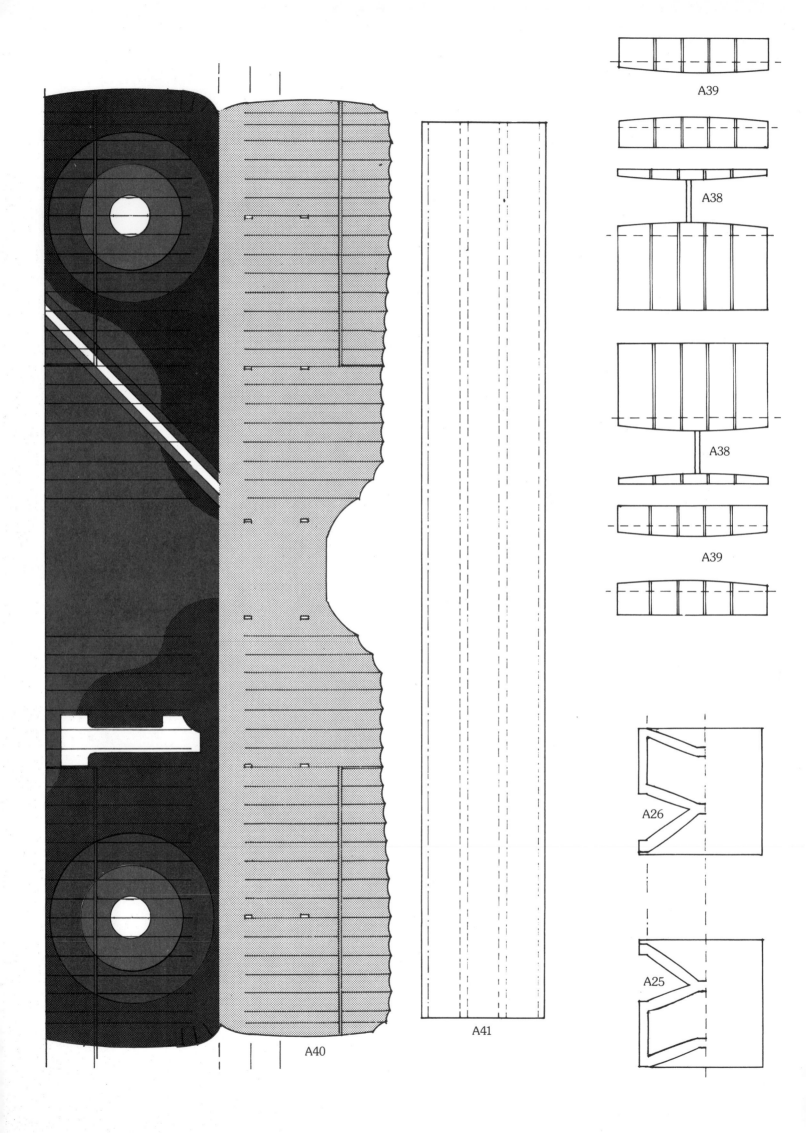

A39

A38

A38

A39

A40

A41

A26

A25

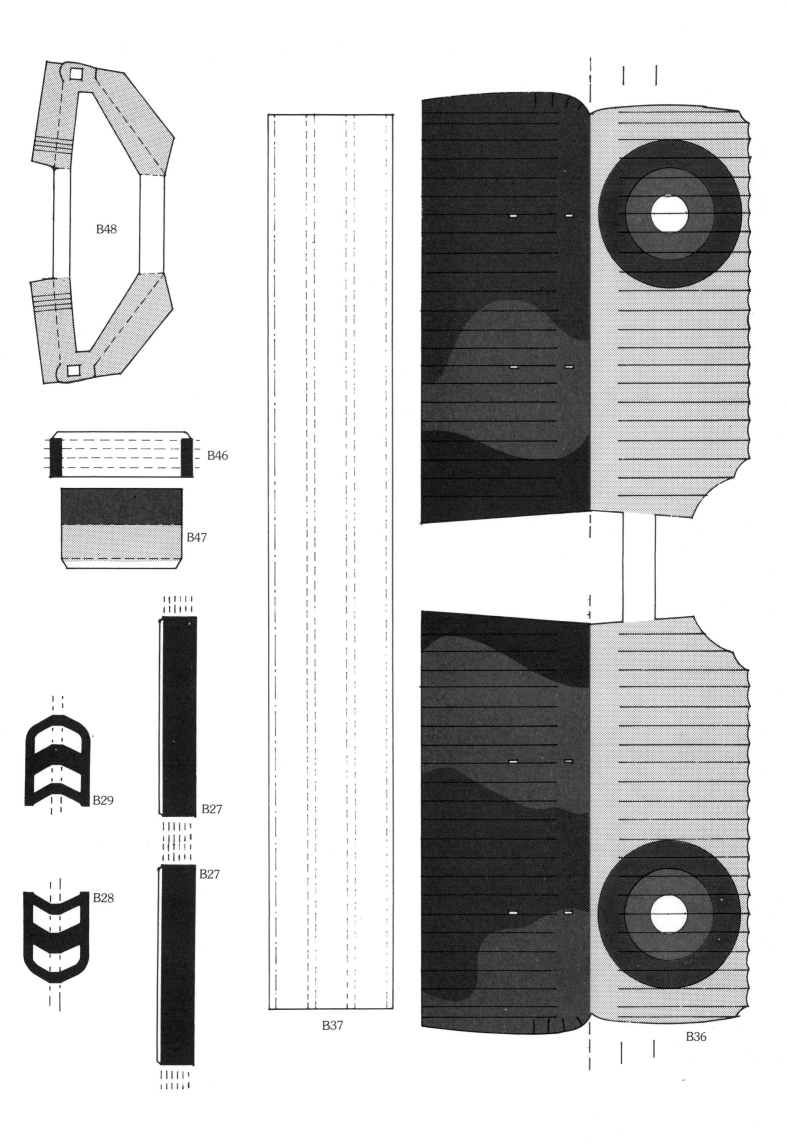

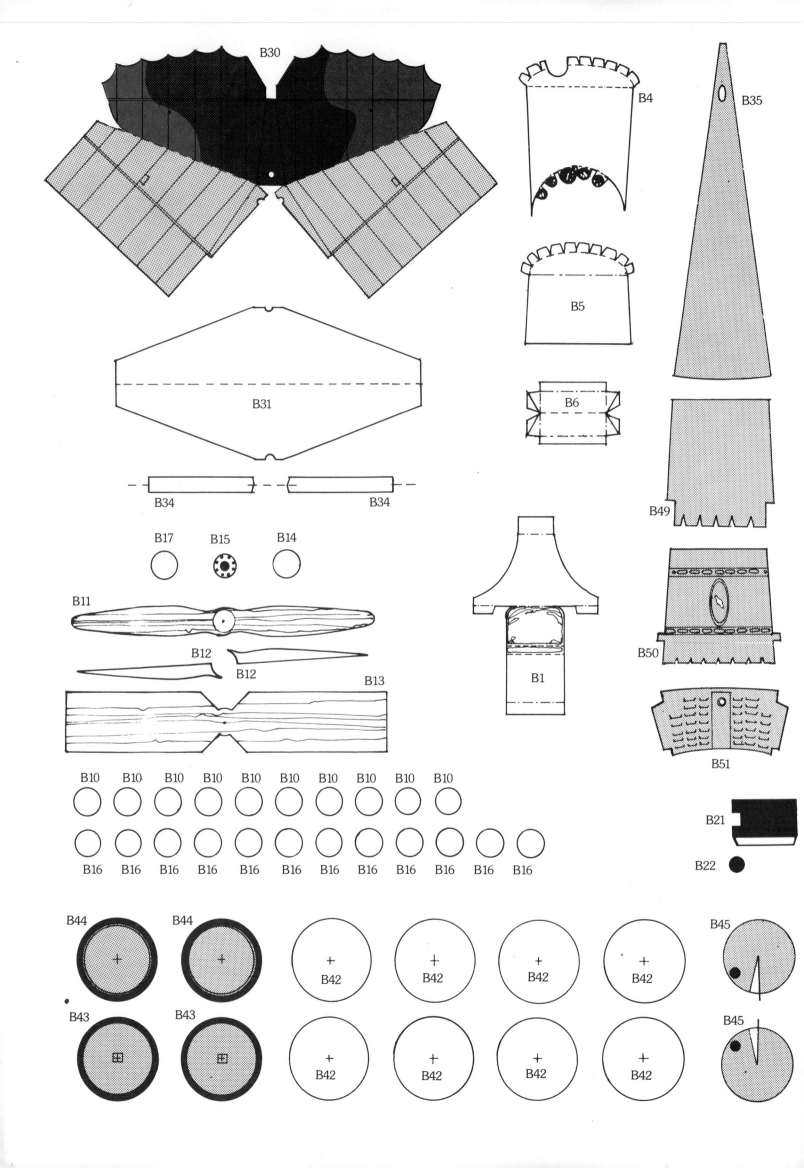

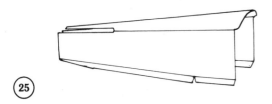

25

Cut out and fold rear fuselage (23).

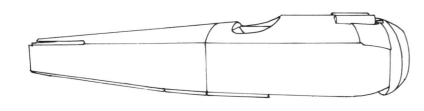

26

Glue into position as shown. When sides are dry, glue upper rear cockpit flaps down. Glue rear bottom tail skid support to side.

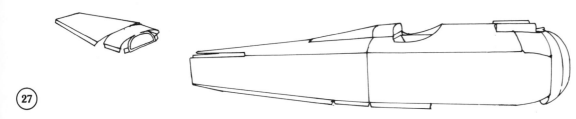

27

Cut out, fold, and glue headrest (24). Glue in position as shown.

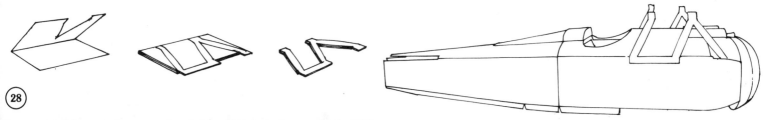

28

Cut out, fold, and glue together left and right cabane struts (25) and (26). When dry, cut out final shapes. Glue in position as shown. Tuck front braces inside front sides.

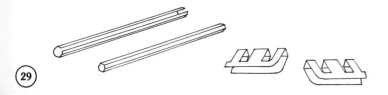

29

Cut out, fold, and glue exhaust pipes (27). Cut out and fold left exhaust collector (28) and right exhaust collector (29).

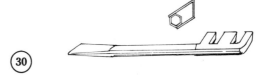

30

Glue an exhaust pipe into each collector as shown. Flatten ends as shown.

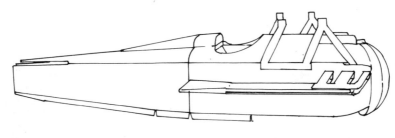

31

Glue collector pipes to sides of fuselage as shown. When dry, glue inside edge of flattened top to side of fuselage.

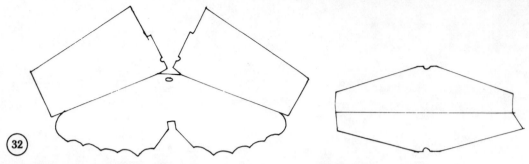

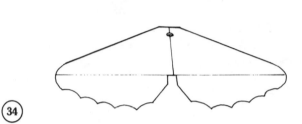

(32)

Cut out and fold stabilizer (30) and stabilizer inner support (31) as shown.

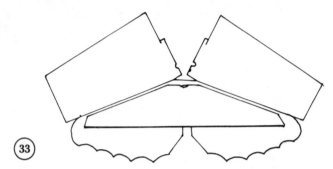

(33)

Glue support together and onto inside of stabilizer as shown.

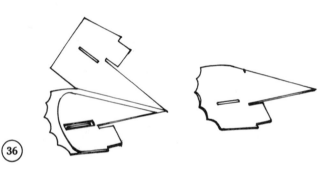

(34)

Close bottom sections, glue to support and along trailing edges. When dry, trim to match top contour.

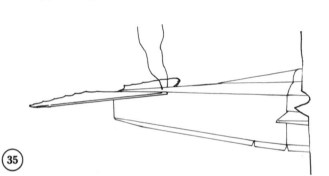

(35)

Thread a 6-inch piece of black thread through holes in top rear of fuselage. Glue stabilizer into position under rear cutout as shown.

(36)

Cut out and fold rudder/fin assembly (32) as shown. Cut out long slots. Glue inner support and outer side as shown.

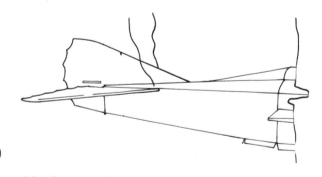

(37)

Glue rudder/fin assembly in position as shown.

(38)

Cut out, fold, and glue rudder control horn (33) as shown.

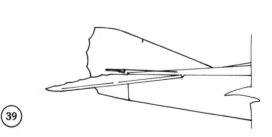

(39)

Glue in position as shown. Glue one end of the thread to the end of each side of the control horn as shown. Trim when dry.

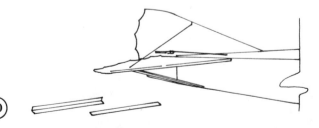

(40)

Cut out, fold over, and glue stabilizer supports (34). Glue in position as shown. Thread a 6-inch piece of black thread through holes in top of stabilizer. Glue center into notch in top of fin. When dry, pull tightly, align fin, and secure each side with a drop of glue. Trim when dry.

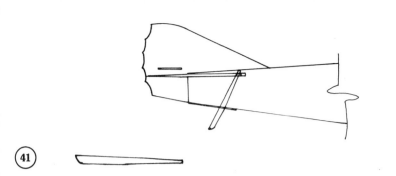

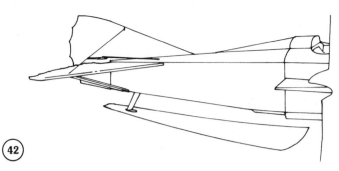

41 Cut a round toothpick to match diagram and glue into hole for tailskid at bottom of fuselage and into hole in stabilizer inside fuselage as shown.

42 Cut out and **gently roll** rear fuselage bottom (35). Glue in place to tabs on **lower sides** as shown.

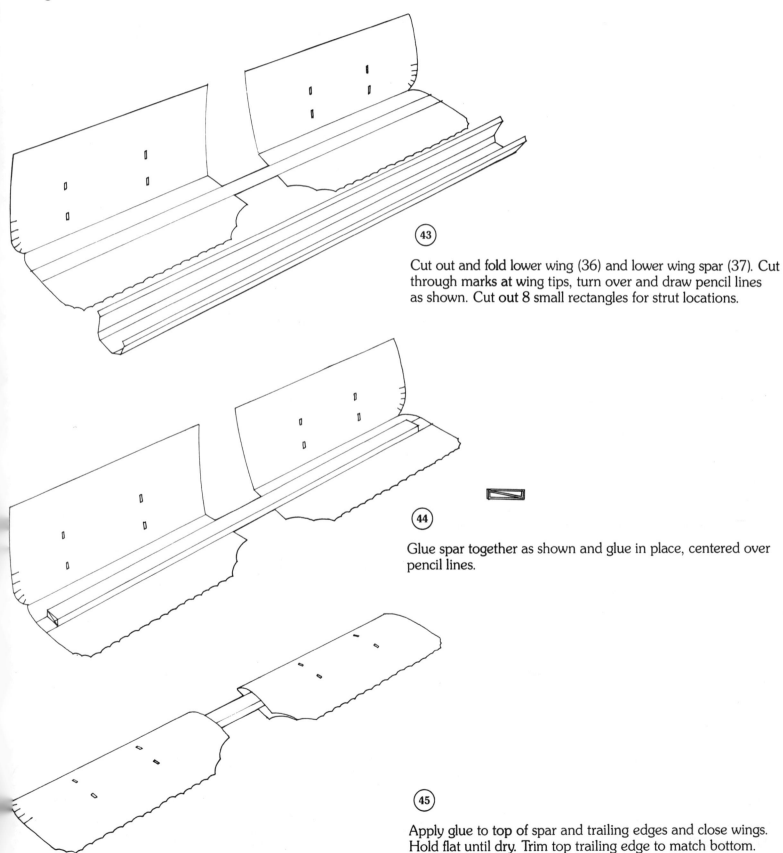

43 Cut out and **fold lower** wing (36) and lower wing spar (37). Cut through **marks at** wing tips, turn over and draw pencil lines as shown. Cut **out 8** small rectangles for strut locations.

44 Glue spar together as shown and glue in place, centered over pencil lines.

45 Apply glue to **top of** spar and trailing edges and close wings. Hold flat until **dry.** Trim top trailing edge to match bottom.

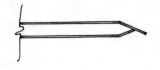

46

Apply glue to wing tips and form top section down as shown, curving forward edges. When dry, trim top overhang to match bottom edge.

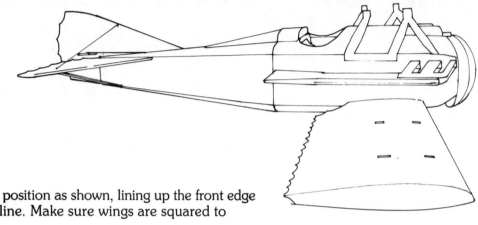

47

Glue lower wing in position as shown, lining up the front edge with fuselage fold line. Make sure wings are squared to fuselage.

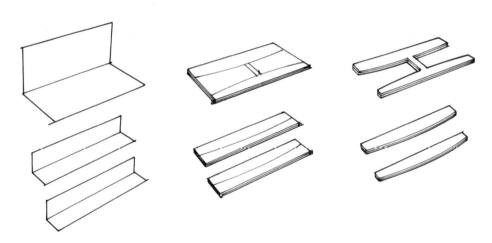

48

Cut out and fold inboard interplane struts (38) and outboard interplane struts (39). Glue together and trim as shown.

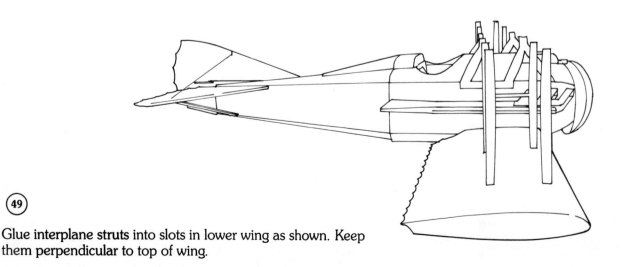

49

Glue interplane struts into slots in lower wing as shown. Keep them perpendicular to top of wing.

12

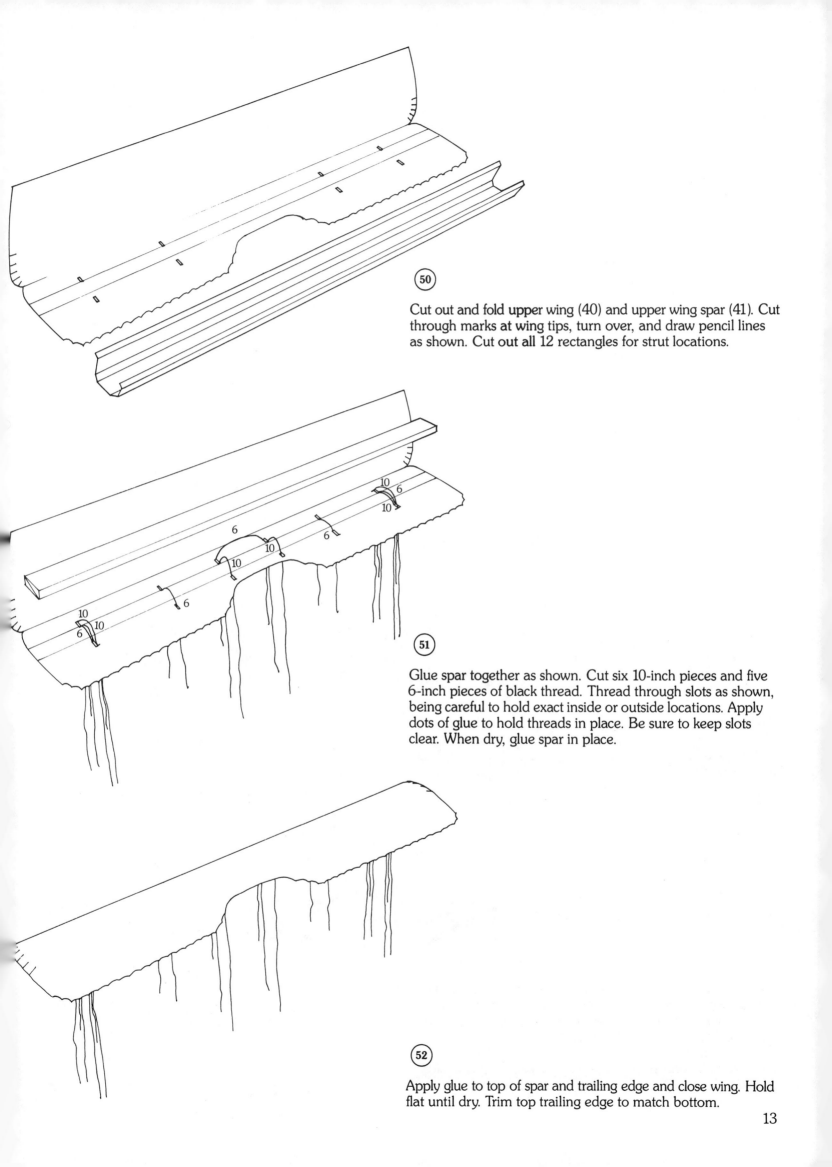

(50)

Cut out and fold upper wing (40) and upper wing spar (41). Cut through marks at wing tips, turn over, and draw pencil lines as shown. Cut out all 12 rectangles for strut locations.

(51)

Glue spar together as shown. Cut six 10-inch pieces and five 6-inch pieces of black thread. Thread through slots as shown, being careful to hold exact inside or outside locations. Apply dots of glue to hold threads in place. Be sure to keep slots clear. When dry, glue spar in place.

(52)

Apply glue to top of spar and trailing edge and close wing. Hold flat until dry. Trim top trailing edge to match bottom.

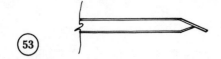

(53) Apply glue to wing tips and form top section down as shown, curving forward edges. When dry, trim top overhang to match bottom edge.

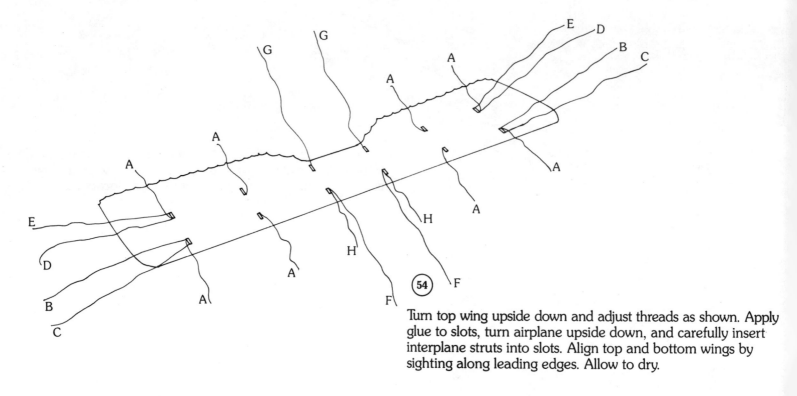

(54) Turn top wing upside down and adjust threads as shown. Apply glue to slots, turn airplane upside down, and carefully insert interplane struts into slots. Align top and bottom wings by sighting along leading edges. Allow to dry.

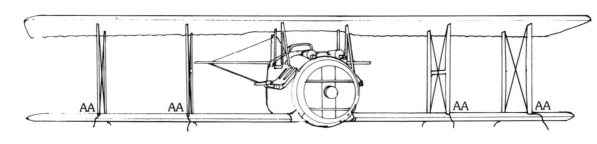

(55) The wing rigging must be done according to the following steps and diagrams. Crossbrace interplane struts. Pull short threads (A) across one another to form an "X," and glue to opposite corners.

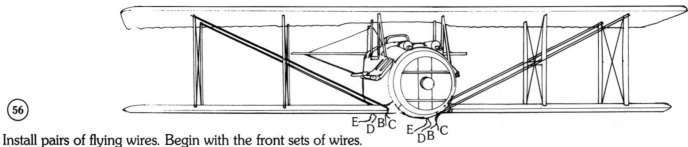

(56) Install pairs of flying wires. Begin with the front sets of wires. Thread inside wires (B) from each end through inboard struts and slide between front wing edge and fuselage. Adjust tension and glue thread into wing/fuselage joint. Pull outside wires (C) along outside of struts and slide along next to first set. Adjust and glue as before. Trim ends when dry. Repeat process for rear sets of wires (D and E), sliding between rear-wing edge and fuselage.

14

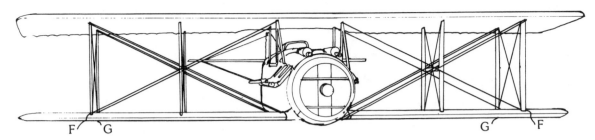

(57) Install landing wires. Thread front wires (F) through inboard struts, pull tight, and glue to base of outboard struts. Repeat for rear wires (G). Trim when dry.

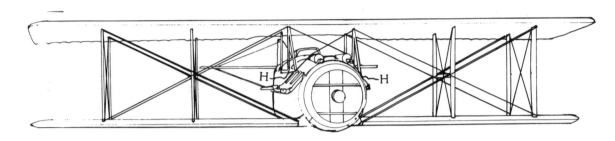

(58) Cross cabane strut wires (H) over machine guns and glue to base of forward struts at opposite sides.

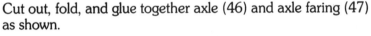

(59) Cut out all 8 center wheel discs (42), inner wheel discs (43), outer wheel discs (44), and covers (45). Glue together as shown. When dry, blacken edges as shown.

(60) Cut out, fold, and glue together axle (46) and axle faring (47) as shown.

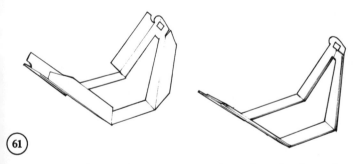

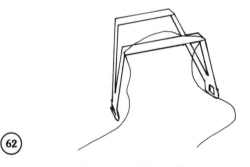

(61) Cut out and fold landing gear (48). Glue flaps back as shown. Trim when dry to match tops.

(62) Insert an 8-inch piece of thread into slots in top front crossbar as shown. Pull tight and glue.

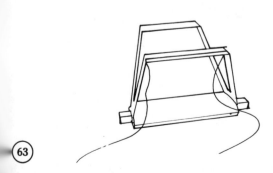

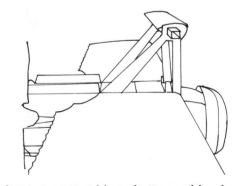

(63) Insert axle ends into landing gear and glue as shown.

(64) Glue landing gear assembly to bottom of fuselage as shown.

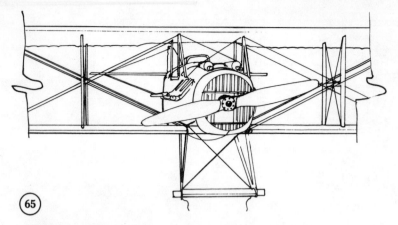

(65) Cross threads and glue to opposite corners of axle. Align axle parallel to wings. Trim when dry.

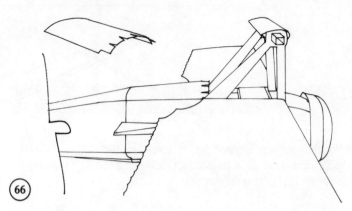

(66) Cut out and gently curve cockpit underside (49). Glue in place to rear section and side tabs as shown.

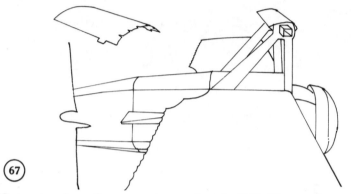

(67) Cut out and gently curve wing underside (50). Glue in place with side tabs inserted in space between front gear strut and wing beam as shown.

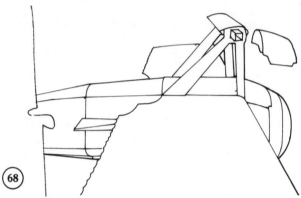

(68) Cut out and roll bottom nose (51). Glue in place with tabs inserted into space between side panels and cockpit structure.

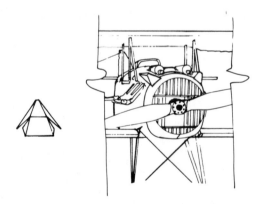

(69) Cut out, fold, and glue left and right camhousing cowls (52 and 53). Glue in place as shown.

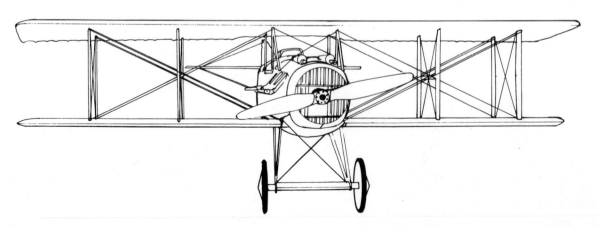

(70) Glue wheels in place, lining up squares on inner wheels with axle ends.

16

Wrapping Gifts Beautifully

Wrapping Gifts Beautifully

Packo Jansen

Sterling Publishing Co., Inc.   New York

English translation © 1991 by Sterling Publishing Company
387 Park Avenue South, New York, N.Y. 10016
Original edition published under the title *Geschenke wunderschön
Verpacken*, © 1990 by Falken-Verlag GmbH
Distributed in Canada by Sterling Publishing
% Canadian Manda Group, P.O. Box 920, Station U
Toronto, Ontario, Canada M8Z 5P9
Distributed in Great Britain and Europe by Cassell PLC
Villiers House, 41/47 Strand, London WC2N 5JE
Distributed in Australia by Capricorn Ltd.
P.O. Box 665, Lane Cove, NSW 2066
Printed in Hong Kong
All rights reserved

Sterling ISBN 0-8069-8456-2

10 9 8 7 6 5 4 3 2 1

Translated by Annette Englander
Edited by Jeanette Green
Photographs by Wolfgang Zöltsch
Illustrations by Daniela Schneider

Library of Congress Cataloging-in-Publication Data

Jansen, Packo. Geschenke wunderschön verpacken. English
    Wrapping gifts beautifully / Packo Jansen.
        p.   cm.
    Translation of: Geschenke wunderschön verpacken. 1990.
    Includes index.
    ISBN 0-8069-8456-2
    1. Gift wrapping.   I. Title.
TT870.J3813   1991
745.54—dc20
                                                            91-14172
                                                            CIP

Contents

The ideas that appear in these pages show a small selection of gift wraps that are created daily by Packo Jansen in Frankfurt, Germany. These gift wraps are assembled step-by-step so that you can easily imitate them.

You'll be able to apply these basic wrapping and decorating techniques again and again. You'll wrap square objects, cover cardboard and attach an object to it, create a ribbon rose, or fold ribbon into a bow and fasten it onto your gift.

These basic techniques are described in detail in the first two chapters, so that you can refer to them when these initial steps are repeated with another wrapping suggestion. After practicing these skills several times, they will become so familiar that you will no longer need to refer to them.

Some wrappings become part of the gift itself, and they may be cherished as a keepsake or reused later: A bow that could be worn in a woman's hair, a ribbon rose that could be fastened onto a suit jacket, a cardboard box to organize small objects, and fabric that could serve as a tablecloth.

Use decorations sparingly, since less is more! Besides, it's important to consider: Who gets what kind of gift, from whom, on what occasion, how and where, and the personality of the receiver. Jansen asks customers these questions and from their answers he creates numerous distinctive wrappings daily. The person who receives the gift recognizes that the gift was not wrapped carelessly and the gift-giver

made a special effort to choose an appropriate presentation.

Before you begin to wrap a gift you consider the *age* and *personality* of the receiver as well as the *occasion*, *presentation* (private or public), and means of *transport*.

For instance, if you present the gift privately, the wrapping may clearly express your feelings. At formal occasions, an open or half-open wrapping allows everyone to see the gift. For airplane or train travel, flat wrappings make sense, but large bows would remain undamaged in your car's back seat.

Considering these aspects helps make the wrapping become part of the gift.

Materials and Tools

The market offers a wealth of gift-wrap paper, foils with prints, and cardboard boxes as well as ribbons in all varieties of quality, size, and color. But why don't you first look into your drawers for leftovers! There you'll certainly find cardboard, tissue paper, velvet, corrugated paper, burlap, and soft or strong fabrics. Also, find single large and small leaves as well as fresh flowers for decoration. You may want to spray some wrappings with whiff of favorite perfume.

When you make bows or fasten your wrappings with ribbons, they should be 2¾ to 6 inches wide. That way they'll look nice and can be used later. Smaller ribbons tend to look less decorative. Many wrapping materials get thrown out immediately after the gift is unwrapped. But other people use and cherish their gift wrap. A nice gift wrap keepsake may be the "stage" of a hydrangea painting or the pedestal of a Chinese vase.

But the presentation itself may include a second small gift; you could hide a piece of jewelry in a box of chocolates and cover

the box or hidden gift within the chocolate box nicely. Or you could fasten a check or money, meant for buying a car, onto a model car.

You'll need just a few simple tools: Ruler, pencil (to mark and pierce holes), scissors, single-sided and double-sided transparent tape, glue stick, and curling ribbon or yarn in various colors.

EDIBLE GIFTS

Box of Chocolates with Rose

"It's my secretary's birthday today," the woman says. "And with all our deadlines, I forgot about it. She's a 28-year-old romantic who has a good aesthetic sense and loves flowers. Here's a box of chocolates; create something with effect!"

Material for a box 14 inches square: Wrapping paper 28 by 40 inches, 6 feet of 4-inch taffeta ribbon, 40 inches of 6-inch tulle, 24 inches of curling ribbon, single-sided and double-sided tape.

1. Place the box near the front of the wrapping paper, as shown, and fold the long sides tightly over the box.

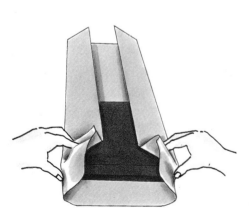

2. With your thumbs and forefingers, press the paper in at the corners of the box.

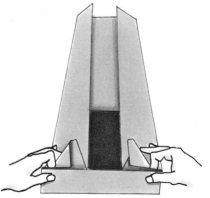

3. Pull the paper up so that its edges lie parallel to those of the box. Then, tighten the paper at the sides to make it level and flush with the box's end.

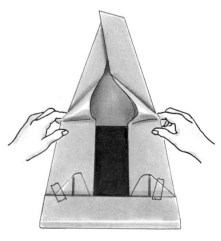

4. Now fold the paper over the box's edge. There will be one paper triangle on the left and another on the right. Tape both edges with single-sided tape. Press the wrapping paper at the box's opposite end inward, so that you create triangular folds.

12

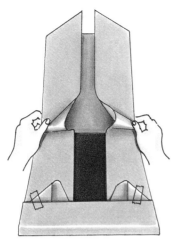

5. Pull up the back of the wrapping paper slowly.

6. Now you can see that the paper triangles lie, as if on their own, on the back edges of the box.

7. Set the box vertically, and pull up the back wrapping of the paper so that its edges are flush with the box's edges.

8. Fold the wrapping paper over and inward about half an inch just in front of the box's top edge. Secure the wrapping paper with double-sided tape to finally seal the package.

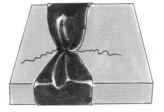

9. Put the taffeta ribbon around the box so that its ends overlap about 3¼ inches, and tie this larger ribbon with curling ribbon.

10. Fold the tulle in half and tie one end into the taffeta ribbon with the thinner, curling ribbon.

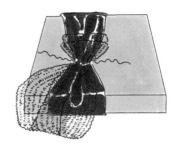

11. Insert the other end of the tulle so that you create a "tulle cloud."

Rose:
40 inches of 4-inch taffeta ribbon, curling ribbon.

1. For the rose, roll one end of taffeta ribbon from left to right diagonally, holding it tightly and firmly, so that you form a stem about 4 to 6 inches long.

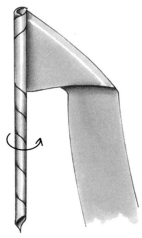

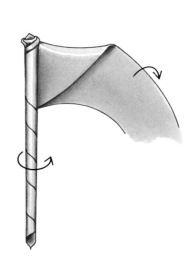

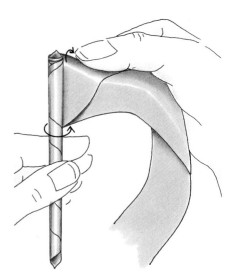

2. Then, holding the stem in your left hand, bend the ribbon's long end backward. You'll create a triangle.

3. Now continue to roll the stem until you almost reach the end of the triangle. You will have created a rosebud.

4. Fold the ribbon on top backward with your right hand to half its width, and wind it around itself once. Place the petal you formed horizontally on the bud. At the same time, hold the stem with your left hand above and turn it from left to right about half a turn.

14

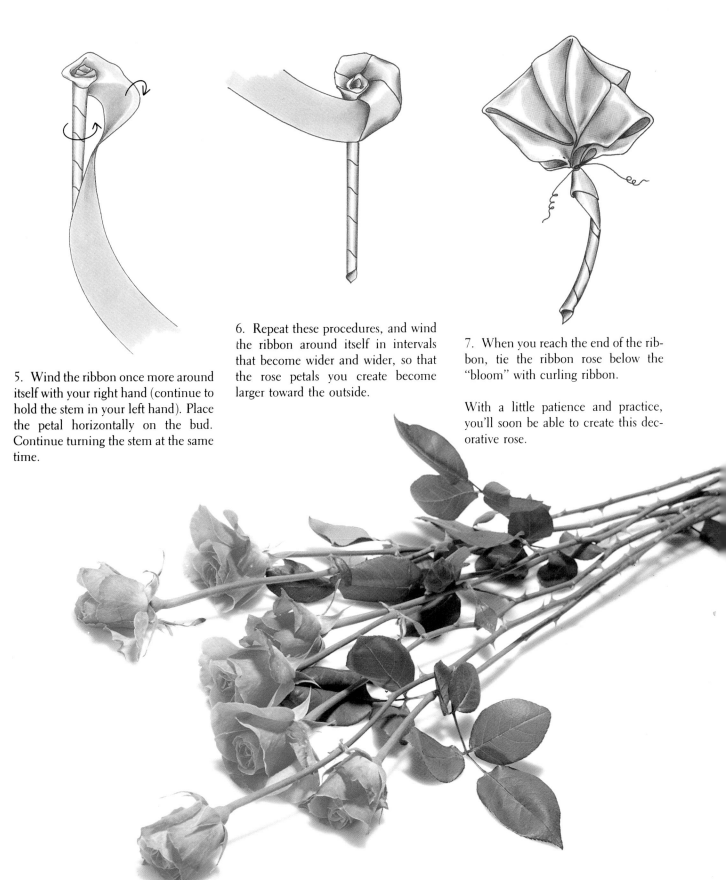

5. Wind the ribbon once more around itself with your right hand (continue to hold the stem in your left hand). Place the petal horizontally on the bud. Continue turning the stem at the same time.

6. Repeat these procedures, and wind the ribbon around itself in intervals that become wider and wider, so that the rose petals you create become larger toward the outside.

7. When you reach the end of the ribbon, tie the ribbon rose below the "bloom" with curling ribbon.

With a little patience and practice, you'll soon be able to create this decorative rose.

Box of Chocolates in Black and Silver

"Our bank manager is very conservative and serious. He despises frippery," our customer declared Monday morning. "The department wants to give him this small gift for his birthday."

Material:
Wrapping paper 3½ times as long and a little wider than the gift, 1 sheet of contrasting paper, single-sided and double-sided tape.

1. Place the gift on top of the paper, and proceed according to steps 2 to 6 on pp. 12 to 13. Then, move the box to a vertical position, and fold the end of the paper into a triangle as shown.

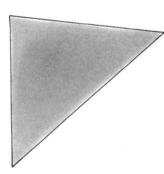

3. Cut out a triangle from the second sheet of contrasting wrapping paper.

2. Pull the paper forward, bending the triangular fold over the front of the package, and then seal the package with double-sided tape.

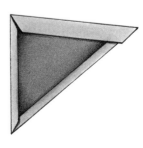

4. Fold the edges about a half inch inward on all three edges of the triangle, and affix it to the package with double-sided tape (see photo).

Box of Chocolates in Black and White

"Our art teacher claims that black and white cannot be considered colors. We want to invite him to see a black-and-white movie. And so that he doesn't get too bored, we hope this colorful mix of chocolates will offer a sweet change."

Material:
Wrapping paper 4½ times as long and a little wider than the gift, 3-inch moiré ribbon as long as the box is wide, single-sided and double-sided ¼-inch tape.

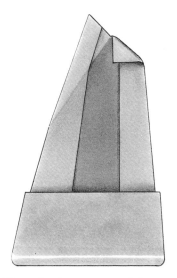

1. Place the box on top of the wrapping paper, and follow steps 2 to 6 on pp. 12 and 13. Flip the box backward, and fold the paper into an acute angle.

einer spitzwinkligen Form.

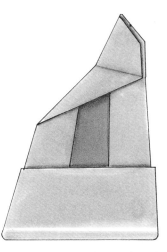

2. Fold the triangle forward with its point inward.

3. Fix the point with single-sided tape inside the paper, taping it to the wrapped package.

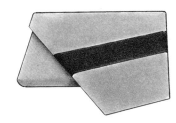

4. Pull the back of the wrapping paper (the "clasp") forward. Place the moiré ribbon across it (as shown), and fasten it to the ribbon's underside with double-sided tape. Seal the finished package with double-sided tape.

Coffee in Burlap Bag

"Our accountant's coffeemaker boiled over today. To cheer him up, we're giving him a pound of coffee as a gift. He's ecologically minded, so fancy wrapping paper is out."

Material:
14 by 40 inches of burlap cloth (from a building supplier), roasted coffee beans, 60 inches of 2 to 4-inch-wide burlap strip, 2 20-inch pieces of 4-inch-wide burlap, curling ribbon.

1. Place the package on top of the burlap cloth.

2. Fold the long sides inward.

3. Then wrap the coffee beans into it.

4. Tie the ends of the burlap strip together with curling ribbon. Leave the end of the coffee purse clasp straight, or fold it into a triangle.

5. Tie the first piece of burlap around the purse, and secure it with curling ribbon, allowing the ends to hang.

6. Fold the ends of the second strip of burlap to form a cross (see illustration).

7. Gather the burlap in the middle, and tie the bow you've created with curling ribbon to the "purse" (see photo).

18

Tea Tin in Japan Paper

"My favorite colleague is leaving for Japan the day after tomorrow. I bought him a tin of green tea as a bonvoyage gift to get him into the right mood for the Orient."

The gift wrap idea: Japan paper decorated with chopsticks. The colleague can use the chopsticks immediately to practice eating sushi.

Material for tea tin containing 5½ to 7 ounces of tea: Tissue paper 20 by 24 inches, Japan paper 20 by 24 inches, 2 20-inch strands of 3½-inch ribbon, curling ribbon, double-sided tape.

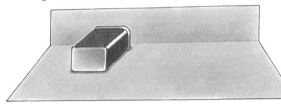

1. Since the wrapping will remain open at the ends, use tissue paper first, folding its long sides over the middle of the tea tin.

2. Then, roll and wrap the can until you reach the end of the paper. Fold in the end about ½ inch, and seal it with double-sided tape.

4. Then wrap the tea tin into it, and fold the end of the paper about ¼ inch inward. Fasten it to the wrapping with double-sided tape.

6. Also fasten the bow to the package, and fasten the second chopstick to the bow. Cut off the leftover curling ribbon.

3. Fold the Japan paper's long sides inward, and place the tea tin on it so that the paper edges jut out left and right about 4 to 6 inches each.

5. First, fold a bow out of ribbon (see p. 18). Then, twist the second ribbon around the middle of the gift box, and secure it with curling ribbon. Push the first chopstick underneath.

19

Bottle with Tuxedo Bow Tie

"This evening we're invited to an eccentric party at an advertising agency. The people are shrill and somewhat crazy," the customer declares. "Their favorite color is violet red, or so I assume, since all their doors are painted in that color."

Material for a bottle of wine: Foil 12 by 48 inches, foil 8 by 16 inches for bow tie, curling ribbon.

1. Place the bottle vertically on the largest piece of foil wrapping paper, and pull the lower edge about 2 inches over the bottle.

3. Roll the bottle from left to right lengthwise into the foil until you nearly reach the end.

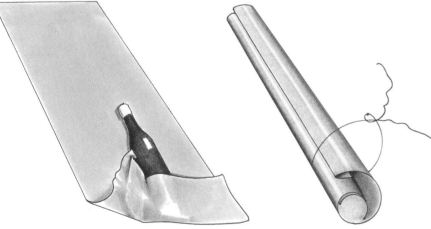

2. Fold the lower left end of the foil toward the bottle.

4. Fold the right end of the foil about ½ inch inward, and seal the package at the base of the bottle with curling ribbon.

7. For the bow tie, fold the right and left ends of the second piece of foil so that they overlap slightly in the middle.

5. Now set the bottle upright, and fold the long foil tube down, curving it around the bottle.

6. Tie the end together with the loose ends of the ribbon already securing the paper at the base of the bottle.

8. Gather the foil in the middle.

Tie the foil tuxedo bow tie you created to the base of the bottle with curling ribbon (see photo).

21

Bottle in Box

"I'm giving my father a bottle of wine to celebrate his completion of a hobby basement. I want to use a large box for the wine since he is very neat and will surely use it. I also don't want to feel guilty that the packaging could end up in the wastebasket."

Material:
Box, tissue paper for lining box, 2 20-inch strands of 3¼-inch ribbon, curling ribbon.

Put the bottle into a box. If the box is too big, stuff it with tissue paper, and close the lid.

Wrap one of the wide ribbons around the box, and tie the ends together with curling ribbon.

Fold a bow out of the second wide ribbon (see p. 18), and fasten it to the first ribbon with curling ribbon.

Bottle in Blue Fabric

Imagine a mild summer evening when your neighbor calls to invite you to a barbecue. In your refrigerator you have a bottle of wine, but your only sheet of wrapping paper is too small to wrap it. But you have some fabric just big enough for your practical neighbor to use later as a tablecloth for her small, round garden table.

Material:
Fabric 48 inches square, 2 20-inch strands of 1¼-inch ribbon, curling ribbon.

1. Fold the fabric square in half.

2. Fold the fabric in half again.

3. Place the folded fabric with the closed point towards you.

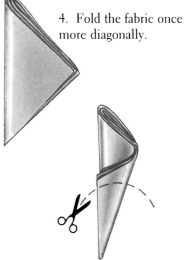

4. Fold the fabric once more diagonally.

5. Fold the fabric again diagonally, and cut the wider, upper edge in a half circle so that the unfolded fabric will look like a flower.

Now place the bottle in the middle of the fabric. Pull the fabric upwards, and tie it at the bottle neck with ribbon, curling ribbon, and a bow (see p. 18).

22

Two Bottles as Firecracker

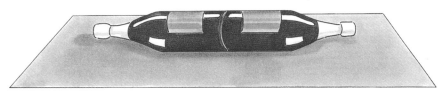

1. Place both bottles with the bottoms facing each other lengthwise in the middle of the largest piece of foil.

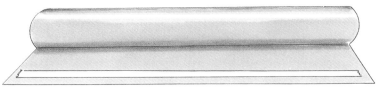

2. Now roll and wrap the foil from back to front tightly around both bottles. Then stick a strip of double-sided tape along the long front edge to seal the package tightly.

3. Gather both foil ends directly next to the bottle tops; then tie them with curling ribbon.

Fasten a tuxedo bow tie made from the smaller two pieces of foil (see p. 20) on each end. In the middle of the bow tie, fasten foil "grass."

"I've been invited to dinner. The menu is supposed to surprise us. So, I don't know what wine or other beverage goes with it, that's why I bought two bottles of champagne. How can I wrap the bottles so that my friends won't immediately recognize what I've brought?"

Material:
Foil 20 by 48 inches, 2 pieces of foil 8 by 20 inches, curling ribbon, strips of foil "grass" (very fine strips), double-sided tape.

23

INTELLECTUAL GIFTS

Book as Purse

"Katrin will soon begin training in a travel agency. To celebrate her new career, I'm giving her this address book. She'll really like it, and it will help her put addresses and telephone numbers in order, instead of being forced to look for scraps of paper."

Material:
Glossy wrapping paper 3½ times as long and a little wider than the gift, 60 inches of 1-inch ribbon, 2-inch ribbon as long as the package is wide, 3 pieces of tulle 4 by 8 inches, curling ribbon, single-sided and double-sided tape.

1. Place the book near the front end of the wrapping paper, and follow steps 2 to 6 on pp. 12 and 13. Tilt the book backwards onto the paper.

2. Now fold the paper's back end to form a point or diagonal.

3. When you fold another corner, then you'll create an asymmetrical form; affix double-sided tape. Do not pull off the backing yet.

4. Place one ribbon around the "purse" flap from inside to outside, and tape it onto the inner side of the flap. Then, tie the long ribbon with curling ribbon inside and around the flap to create a strap.

5. On the outer side, fasten curling ribbon onto the "purse flap" ribbon and work 2 pieces of tulle into it. Tie the third piece of tulle onto the "purse strap" ribbon.

Open Book Wrap

Martin has completed his apprenticeship as a bookbinder with honors. He wants to dedicate his journeyman piece, a carefully crafted address book, to his master. "I want to present him the book in a way that everyone can see it."

Material:
Sturdy square of cardboard big enough for an open book to fit diagonally; glossy wrapping paper 2½ times as long as and 4 inches wider than the cardboard, 2 pieces of tulle 4 inches square, curling ribbon (length depends on that of the gift), single-sided and double-sided tape, sharp pencil.

1. Place the cardboard on the glossy wrapping paper. Fold the long sides tightly over the cardboard or tape them on.

2. Then fold the lower paper edge over the cardboard and affix with tape. Fold the sheet's back part about ½ inch inward, then tilt it forward over the lower end of the paper, and fasten it to the cardboard with double-sided tape.

3. Place the open book diagonally on the smooth side of the cardboard. Mark two holes each close to the book's upper and lower edges, and prick them into the cardboard with a sharp pencil. Pull the curling ribbons through the pairs of holes, and tie a knot on top of the book (usually you'd tie the knot on the back side of the cardboard), to keep it in place. Let the ribbon ends hang!

From the wide ribbons fold two bows (see p. 18), and tie them tightly to the book with curling ribbon.
 Tie tulle into the middle of each bow. Cut off the loose ends of curling ribbon.

Picture as Stage

"My sister loves hydrangeas more than anything else. By accident, I discovered this wonderful old hydrangea painting."

What was more obvious than presenting the painting to her in matching paper and placing the gift for viewing on an open "stage" built from corrugated cardboard.

Material for a small painting:
Sturdy cardboard 12 by 17½ inches, glossy paper 28 by 40 inches, 20 inches of 3¼-inch ribbon, tulle 40 by 6 inches, curling ribbon (length depends on that of the gift), single-sided and double-sided tape, sharp pencil.

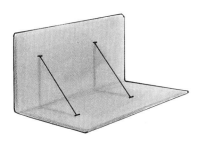

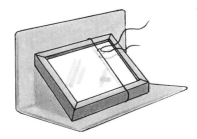

1. Cover the cardboard loosely with glossy paper (see p. 28), and fold it in the middle to create a 90 degree angle which you will stabilize. Punch 2 holes each in upper and lower sides of the cardboard; the distance between the holes should be not quite as wide as the painting frame. Then pull 2 pieces of curling ribbon through them. Tie curling ribbons on the cardboard's back side.

2. Lean the painting against the ribbons, and pull another ribbon through one of the pairs of holes. This will keep the painting in place.

3. Create a bow from wide ribbon and another bow from tulle, and fasten both to the curling ribbon (see p. 18).

CD as Gable

"My husband only wants compact discs for gifts. I'd like very much to surprise him for a change."

The customer will be able to surprise him with a CD wrapped in the shape of a house gable. Colors here—green and gold—would suit a Christmas oratorio or brighten reggae hits.

Material for a CD:
Sturdy corrugated cardboard 5½ by 11¼ inches, opaque foil 28 by 40 inches, 2 20-inch strands of 3½-inch ribbon, curling ribbon, single-sided and double-sided tape, sharp pencil.

1. Set the CD on end vertically in the middle of the corrugated cardboard. With the pencil, punch 2 holes into the right and left edge of the cardboard. Pull the curling ribbon through the holes, and tie the ribbon on the underside (see p. 28). Now place the CD cardboard diagonally on the foil.

2. Fold the long edges up one over the other, to shape a triangular roof and secure them with double-sided tape.

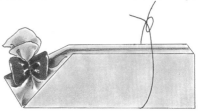

3. Gather the right and left edges half way up the "gable," tie them with curling ribbon, and decorate with bows (see p. 18 and photo below).

Record to Look Into

"My colleague is an expert on jazz. I have found an old, rare Dave Brubeck album for him. His birthday will be celebrated at an Easter morning jazz pint-brunch."

So that the colleague doesn't have to unwrap the gift in the bustle of the jam session, but will be able to recognize the gift in its wrappings, this package has an inside view.

Material:
Glossy wrapping paper 20 by 28 inches, 1 piece of contrasting paper, single-sided and double-sided tape.

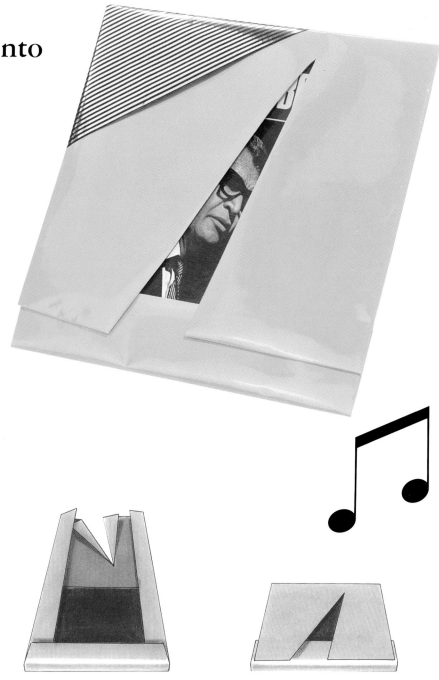

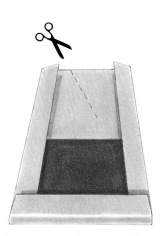

1. Place the record on top of the wrapping paper. Fold the long sides inward, then pull the front paper edge back over the record, and tape it onto the long sides. Make a cut about seven-eighths into the paper as shown.

2. Fold the paper on the left and right from the cut inward to form a narrow, pointy wedge. Fix the triangles so formed with double-sided tape.

3. Stick a strip of double-sided tape near the edge left and right of the wedge, and close the wrapping.

Cut a triangle from contrasting paper. Fold the edges inside, and attach the paper with double-sided tape onto the back of the LP (see photo).

Record Cover to Reuse

"My brother-in-law will receive a record from me for his birthday. He's a thrifty person who doesn't throw anything away." With this wrapping, he won't have to throw away anything. He can easily pull off the ribbon and remove the record. The cover and decorative wrap can be reused.

Material:
Glossy wrapping paper 20 by 28 inches, 2 strands of 3¼-inch ribbon—one 30 inches and one 24 inches long, curling ribbon, double-sided tape.

1. Place the record on the wrapping paper as shown. Fold the upper right corner inward, and slide it under the LP.

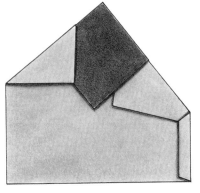

2. Fold the upper left corner over the record.

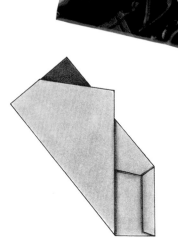

3. Fold the lower left corner over the LP, and fold the triangle that juts out flush with the record's edge. Do not tape it on!

4. Fold the large lower triangle over the LP; then fold the point that juts out inward flush with the edge, and secure it with double-sided tape.

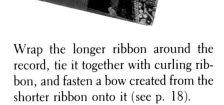

Wrap the longer ribbon around the record, tie it together with curling ribbon, and fasten a bow created from the shorter ribbon onto it (see p. 18).

Record with Funnel

"In Salzburg we heard Mozart's flute and piano concerto. The performance was wonderful. I'm giving my wife this record, recorded at the same concert."

Material:
Glossy paper 28 by 40 inches, 2 strands of 4-inch ribbon—one 30 inches and one 20 inches long, curling ribbon, single-sided and double-sided tape.

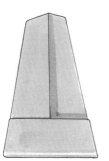

1. Place the record on top of the wrapping paper. First fold the long sides inward.

3. From the right upper corner, roll the wrapping paper diagonally forward so that you create a small funnel.

Wrap the longer ribbon around the package, and fasten a bow created from the shorter ribbon (see p. 18) with curling ribbon.

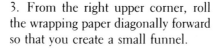

2. Then fold the lower edge up parallel to the LP, and tape it on the long sides with double-sided tape.

4. Pull the paper flap with the funnel over the LP, and secure it with double-sided tape.

33

WEARABLE GIFTS

Sweater as Bow

The customer knitted her husband a sweater. "Actually, my husband thinks that any gift wrap is wasteful, but nevertheless, I've brought this leftover fabric, since he could use it later as a cover for our bird cage."

Material:
Fabric 30 by 40 inches, fabric strip 10 to 20 inches, yarn, gift card.

1. Flatten the sweater, then fold it to a width of 16 inches, and place the arms in a zigzag on top.

3. Fold the front and back part of the fabric over the sweater to create a package.

2. Now fold the sweater to 10 inches long, and place it on the fabric. Pull the fabric first from the left and then from the right over the sweater.

4. Fold the fabric strip to create a narrow band. Tie the band tightly around the middle of the package.

Tie the fabric strip's ends (one atop another) together with yarn. The package becomes a large bow. Fasten a note card to the bow with yarn or curling ribbon.

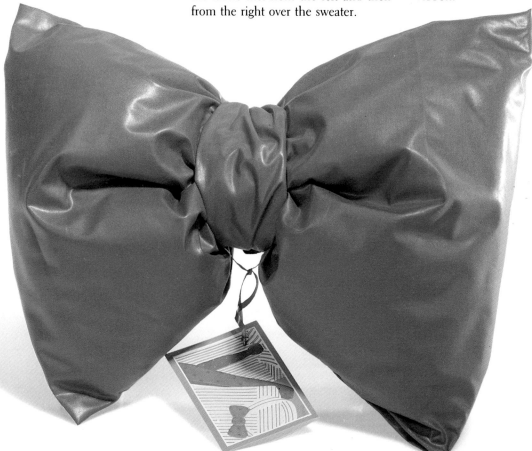

Sweater as Water Lily

"Could you quickly wrap this sweater for me?" the customer asked. "I nearly forgot my niece's birthday. Like most young people, she likes bright colors. She also loves flowers."

Material:
Foil 24 inches square, curling ribbon.

Rose: 40 inches of 4-inch ribbon.

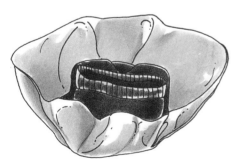

1. Fold the sweater, and place it in the middle of the wrapping foil with its neck and shoulders held vertically. Pull the foil up from all sides so that it surrounds the sweater.

2. Tie the foil together on top—with the sweater neck and shoulders peering out—with curling ribbon.

3. Arrange the sweater still visible like a water lily. Place a rose made from ribbon in the middle (see pp. 14 and 15).

Although you can see part of the gift, you cannot quite recognize what it is.

Tie in Long Case

"My business partner has a tie fetish," the young customer declared. "Every day he wears a different one. Since he can take a joke, I bought him this old number at a flea market."

Material for the case:
Sturdy cardboard 3¼ by 27½ inches, glossy paper 10 by 32 inches, wrapping paper 16 by 32 inches, 2 strands of 2¾-inch ribbon—one 10 inches and one 20 inches long, tulle 4 inches square, curling ribbon, double-sided tape, sharp pencil.

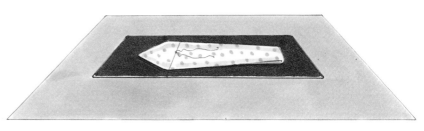

1. Cover the cardboard with glossy paper. Place the tie on it, fold the tie in half and secure it with curling ribbon (see p. 28). Then, place the cardboard horizontally on the sheet of wrapping paper.

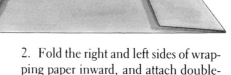

2. Fold the right and left sides of wrapping paper inward, and attach double-sided tape.

4. Starting with the paper's back edge, create an obtuse triangle point by folding left and right sides of the wrapping paper (as shown). Attach double-sided tape to the paper's lower edge.

3. Fold the front wrapping paper edge over the tie and tape it down.

5. Tape the triangle to the paper's lower edge. Wrap the short ribbon around the case, and tie it together with curling ribbon, then fasten a bow made from the shorter wide ribbon (see p. 18). Into this bow you could work a contrasting ribbon, and tie the final bow together with curling ribbon.

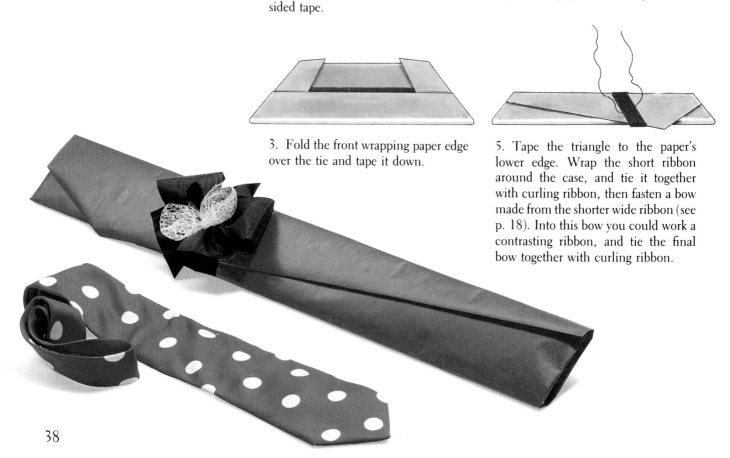

Tie in Envelope

The customer discovered a tie for her husband when she was shopping in the city: "I liked it so much that I just had to buy it."

Since the tie's color matched the dress the customer wore, I chose the same color for the gift wrapping.

Material:
Wrapping paper 14 by 28 inches, 2 20-inch strands of 3¼-inch ribbon, curling ribbon, double-sided tape.

1. Create an envelope by first folding the long sides about ½ inch inward.

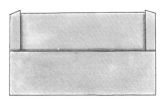

2. Fold the front edge about 6 inches backward, and close it up with double-sided tape to create a pocket.

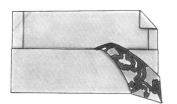

3. Put the tie in the pocket, and fold the back corners of the paper inward.

4. Fold the upper paper edge inward and attach double-sided tape.

5. Close the envelope.

Don't worry: The tape can easily be detached from the tie, and it won't leave a mark.

Wrap the shorter ribbon around the envelope; tie it with curling ribbon. Then make a bow from the longer ribbon (see p. 18), and fasten it to the other ribbon with curling ribbon.

Tie in "Sketchbook"

"My uncle loves roses more than anything else," the customer told me. "He
paints them, grows them, and gave me
a wonderful bouquet of dried roses not
long ago. I've found a rose tie for him.
The wrapping should be artful."

Material:
Sturdy cardboard 12 inches square, 2
sheets of glossy wrapping paper 20 by
28 inches, card and envelope, double-
sided ¾-inch tape.

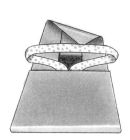

1. Cover the cardboard with glossy
wrapping paper (see p. 28). Then attach the envelope to it with tape, and
place it on the second sheet of glossy
paper.

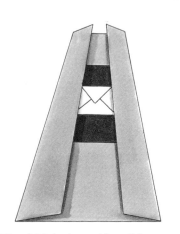

2. First fold the long sides of the paper
inward.

4. Fold the paper's back edge from left
to right. Bend the created flap forward.

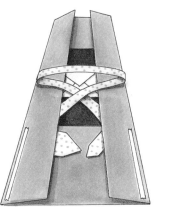

3. Then slide the wide edges of the tie
under the paper's edges, and attach
double-sided tape on the outside, as
shown.

5. Attach double-sided tape diagonally
on the outside along the entire width
of the package as shown. Do not de-
tach the backing on the tape yet. Pull
the tie's narrow part tightly to the outside, and then fasten it to the double-
sided tape.

   Don't worry: The tape can easily be
detached from the tie, and it doesn't
leave any marks.

Nightgown in Red and Black

We're spending a romantic weekend in Paris. "Since she loves to wear silk, I have chosen this nightgown. The wrapping should be extravagant and in her favorite colors, red and black."

Material:
Gift box 12½ inches square and 2 inches deep, tulle 4 by 40 inches, curling ribbon.

Rose:
40 inches of 4-inch ribbon.

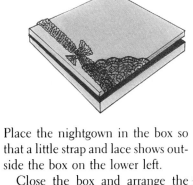

Place the nightgown in the box so that a little strap and lace shows outside the box on the lower left.

Close the box and arrange the lace on top of the lid. Now wrap tulle around the box, and tie it with curling ribbon. Fasten the ribbon roses onto it (see pp. 14 and 15).

41

ACCESSORIES

Perfume Openly Wrapped

"My wife is a designer, and I promised to have someone create her very own personal perfume. I found this beautiful small perfume bottle which is perfect for it."

Material for small bottle 1¼ by 1½ by 4 inches:
2 pieces of sturdy cardboard 3⅗ by 14 inches, 2 strips of glossy paper—one 7 by 16 inches and one 5¼ by 17¾ inches, 3 pieces of tulle 4 inches square, curling ribbon, double-sided tape, sharp pencil.

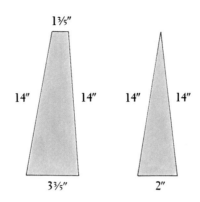

1. Cut cardboard into 2 long wedges. See illustration for shapes and sizes.

2. Then cut the glossy paper for each cardboard sheet and cover both. For the wedge with the pointy top use 17¾-inch-long paper; the edge will jut out about 2¾ inches at the bottom.

3. Fasten the upper wedge to the lower wedge with double-sided tape. This way, both parts will be flexible when attached to each other.

4. Attach the bottle of perfume onto the lower wedge with curling ribbon (see p. 28). Then pierce a hole with the pencil in front of the bottle. Stick the tulle into this hole.

Fix the upper wedge point to the top of the bottle stopper with double-sided tape.

Brooch in "Goblet"

"Do gift-wrapping services simply use foil and glossy paper, or could they use more environmentally friendly wrappings? Surely you'll have a good idea for wrapping this brooch."

Material:
Stretchable corrugated cardboard used to pack wine bottles, tissue paper or silk 6 by 8 inches, 2¾-inch tulle, curling ribbon.

Rose:
40 inches of 4-inch ribbon.

1. Stretch the corrugated paper's lower edge wide enough to create a surface to stand on.

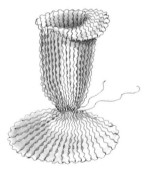

2. Tie the "stand" together with curling ribbon, and attach a ribbon rose (see pp. 14 and 15) and tulle. Turn the corrugated paper's upper edge inside out, and place tissue paper or silk fabric into the goblet. Fasten the brooch to the paper or fabric.

Later you could use the goblet as a shelf decoration.

45

Ring in Apple

"Tomorrow is our first wedding anniversary," says the young man. "This ring must be wrapped uniquely. I want my wife to unwrap the ring with suspense." Since he told us that his wife likes apples, this idea emerged.

Material:
Apple, sturdy corrugated cardboard 8 inches square, wrapping paper 14 inches square, 2 pieces of tulle 8 by 4 inches, curling ribbon, small plastic bag, sharp pencil, paring knife.

First put the ring in the plastic bag; then slice or break the apple in half. Remove the core. Hide the ring in one hollowed out apple half, and place the other half on top.

Cover the cardboard with wrapping paper, and tie the apple onto it with curling ribbon (see p. 28).

Work tulle into the curling ribbon.

You won't be able to see that the apple is cut in half.

Ring in Box of Chocolates

Here the intention is to throw the recipient off track. This works best for someone with a good sense of humor, since she may be disappointed receiving yet another box of chocolates instead of the hoped-for ring.

Material:
Box of chocolates, wrapping paper, tissue paper or cellophane to cover 1 candy, double-sided tape.

Take out one piece of chocolate candy and put the ring in the empty space. Or place the ring around a chocolate wrapped with tissue paper or cellophane. If you don't mind the chocolate mess, you could stick it into a chocolate.

   After you close the box, wrap it so that it's easily recognizable as a box of chocolates. Wrap it simply (cf. p. 16).

47

Evening Purse Half Hidden

"The woman I'm seeing has wanted a beaded evening bag for a long time, but she doesn't like modern ones. I've found an expensive one from an antique dealer. I want everyone at the birthday party to see how much trouble I took with this special gift."

Material:
Sturdy cardboard 16 by 20 inches, glossy wrapping paper 28 by 40 inches, 24 inches of 2¾-inch foil ribbon, curling ribbon, double-sided tape, sharp pencil.

Rose:
40 inches of 4-inch ribbon.

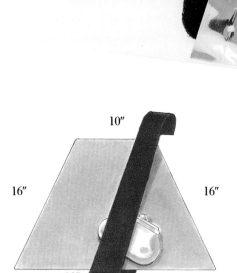

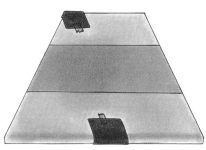

1. Cut the cardboard to the measurements shown, and cover it with the glossy paper (see p. 28). Set the purse on the cardboard, and place the foil ribbon over it.

2. Fix the foil ends to the cardboard's underside with double-sided tape.

3. Fasten ribbon roses (see pp. 14 and 15) on the cardboard with curling ribbon by punching holes in it with a pencil.

Wristwatch in Star Paper

"Our son wanted a good wristwatch with a glowing face and with date and moon phase indicators. He occupies most of his spare time with astronomy." The wrapping I chose looks like a sky filled with stars, comet tails, and rising moons.

Material:
Sturdy cardboard 10 by 14 inches, wrapping paper 14 by 32 inches, paper strip 4 by 13¼ inches, curling ribbon, single-sided and double-sided tape, sharp pencil.

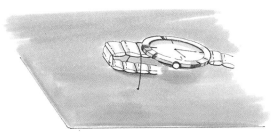

1. Cover the cardboard with wrapping paper, and tie the watch onto it with curling ribbon (see p. 28).

2. Fold the paper strip in on the long sides so that it's narrower at one end. Then fold the paper's front and back edges inward, and fasten them with tape.

3. Place the paper strip diagonally above the watch so that it remains partially visible, and secure both paper edges underneath the cardboard with double-sided tape.

PLAYFUL GIFTS

Hippopotamus in Jungle Cardboard Box

"Matthew is 6 years old, and his favorite animals are hippopotamuses. We found a cuddly new cloth hippo. The gift should be easy to open, since Matt is impatient. If you use a sturdy box, he could use it later as a play chest for small toys."

Material:
Box just big enough for the toy, tissue paper or see-through foil to line the box, 2¼-inch ribbon a few inches longer than the lid, 3 pieces of tulle 6 by 12 inches, curling ribbon or yarn, double-sided tape.

Cover the box's inside with tissue paper or foil (here the box becomes a river bed) and place the cloth animal in it.

Wrap the ribbon across the length of the lid, and fasten it on both ends inside the lid with double-sided tape.

Fasten pieces of tulle with curling ribbon or yarn to the top of the lid. Place the lid on the box.

Bear with Bow

Theresa bought an adorable teddy bear for the man she's seeing. "He can hug the bear instead of me when I have to work overtime."

Theresa put the bear into a nostalgic box. "Now Michael will no longer have the excuse that he doesn't have a useful prop for our vacation photos."

Material:
Box, 4-inch ribbon to tie the box, 2 20-inch strands of 2¾-inch ribbon, curling ribbon.

Put the bear in the box so that at least its head shows. Cover two-thirds of the box with the lid. Wrap the longer ribbon around the box and lid. Fasten the ribbon with curling ribbon, and tie a bow created from another wide ribbon (see p. 18) onto it.

Tie a second bow to a long piece of curling ribbon, and fasten it around the bear's neck.

Train as Candy Chain

"I'm giving my godchild Jennifer a wooden train for Christmas since girls like to play with trains as much as boys do."

So that Jennifer doesn't guess what's inside the package immediately, we wrapped the toy train like a candy chain. The engine and each car become surprises when she unwraps them one by one.

Material for a 4-part toy train:
Packing foam or newspapers, foil or fabric 48 by 60 inches, 5 pieces of foil 8 inches square, curling ribbon.

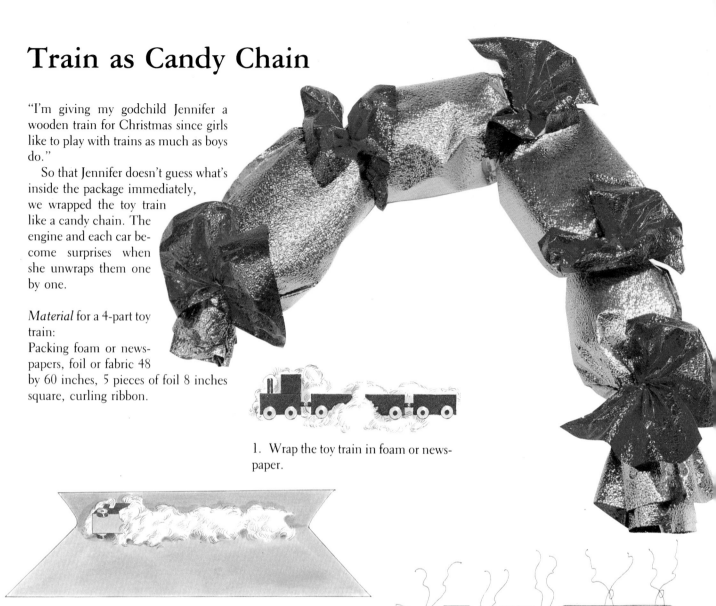

1. Wrap the toy train in foam or newspaper.

2. Then roll the whole thing into the foil.

3. Fasten curling ribbon at each end and between cars. Then squeeze the five foil squares together from both sides to create bows, and fasten them onto the candy chain train with curling ribbons.

Harmonica Half Hidden

"My sister is going to Martha's Vineyard for a few weeks this summer. She's taking her red bicycle, red backpack, and a bright red lightweight tent. She used to play harmonica. Maybe she'll want to play it again on vacation."

Material:
Corrugated cardboard 7 by 14 inches, glossy wrapping paper 16 by 34 inches, curling ribbon, sheet music, single-sided and double-sided tape, sharp pencil.

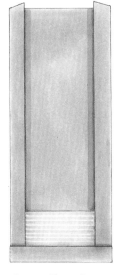

1. Place the cardboard on top of the glossy wrapping paper, toward the front. Fold the long side in as shown. Then fold the front edge back and fasten it with tape.

2. Bend the cardboard rearward once, and lay it on the wrapping paper.

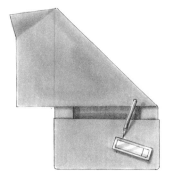

3. Place the harmonica on the paper, and fasten it with curling ribbon (see p. 28). Fold the paper's upper part diagonally from right to left, and leave about ¾ inch of space between the paper's edge and the cardboard's edge.

4. Fold the paper inward that juts out on the left to create a flush edge.

5. Pull the triangle created from the left upper side over the harmonica, and attach it to the cardboard's underside.

Push the sheet music under the mouth organ.

PRACTICAL GIFTS

Coffeemaker with Hearts

"We are invited to my cousin's wedding. The couple would like a coffeemaker. We'll be taking it with us to the wedding in a fully packed car. I'd like a simple, but loving wedding wrap."

Material:
Glossy paper (size depends on that of the gift), 4-inch ribbon (length depends on gift's circumference), 32 inches of 4-inch ribbon, single-sided and double-sided tape, glue stick, coffee beans.

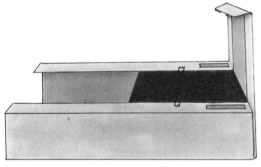

1. Wrap the coffeemaker in its original box. Measure the wrapping paper so that when the long sides are folded inward, each side lies about 1¼ inches on the box. Then put double-sided tape on the sides. Pull the paper's right part up, and fold the edges inward. Fold the upper edge about ½ inch inward, and tape it to the box.

2. Do the same thing on the box's other side, and also fold the paper's upper edge in ½ inch.

3. Use double-sided tape to fix the paper onto the package. This will be the package's underside.

4. "Draw" with the glue stick two intertwined hearts on the smooth upper side of the wrapped box. Put coffee beans on the hearts and press them down. Wrap the broad ribbon around the package horizontally. Tie this ribbon together with curling ribbon, and work a bow you've created into it (see p. 18).

Pocket Calculator Half Hidden

"Our friend is the new owner of a Hard Rock Cafe. I'm giving him this pocket calculator at the opening. Then maybe bookkeeping will be easier, since mental arithmetic has never been his strong point."

Material:
Sturdy cardboard 2 times as long and 3 times as wide as the object, glossy wrapping paper 2 inches wider and over 2 times longer than the cardboard, 1 long strip of glossy paper, curling ribbon, double-sided tape, sharp pencil.

1. Cover the cardboard with glossy paper, and attach the calculator (see p. 28).

2. Fold the long sides of the glossy paper strip inward, and attach its ends to the cardboard's back side with double-sided tape.

Juicer with Fruit

"My husband's colleague is getting married. We bought this pretty juicer, and we want to wrap it not too daringly but uniquely."

The juicer will remain in its original box for the wrap we've devised.

Material:
Glossy wrapping paper (size depends on that of the gift), 4-inch ribbon (length depends on gift's circumference), 32 inches of 4-inch ribbon, 3 pieces of cellophane, curling ribbon, double-sided tape.

Orange, lemon, grapefruit, single leaves for decoration.

1. Place the gift on the wrapping paper and follow steps 1 to 3 on p. 58. Wrap the ribbon around the box, and tie it together on top of the box with curling ribbon. Insert a bow created from the 32-inch length of ribbon—cross the ribbon ends and gather them in the middle (see steps 6 and 7, p. 18). Attach the bow with curling ribbon to the ribbon wrapped around the package.

2. Wrap the fruits individually in cellophane, tying them closed with curling ribbon. Attach them to the middle of the bow with curling ribbon.

Fasten leaves to the bow.

Juicer as Orange

"Our son and his friend have decided to live together. Both like freshly squeezed orange juice. That's why we're giving the couple this chrome juicer at their house-warming party."

Material for an object 8 inches cube: Fabric 32 inches square; excelsior, packing wool, or fine wood shavings; curling ribbon; leaves.

1. Spread the fabric and pack about half of the excelsior tightly in the middle. Set the juicer on it.

2. Pull the fabric up on all four corners, and hold it together loosely with one hand. With the other hand fill in the remaining excelsior, and spread it out to create an orange shape. It's easier to do this with two people.

Tie the "orange" together with curling ribbon, and stick green leaves under the ribbon.

Clock Radio as Radio

"Something really stupid happened to me," a regular customer said. "I left my son's birthday present, a clock radio, in a store while I was shopping. Unfortunately, no one turned it in, so I had to buy a second one. Wrap this one wittily."

After some deliberation, we found a solution. The gift wrap should indicate that the customer bought the same present twice.

Material:
Wrapping paper 3 times as long and a little wider than the gift, long wooden stick, aluminum foil, 1 square of perforated ribbon, 1 square of black glossy foil the same size as the perforated ribbon, 6 buttons, single-sided and double-sided tape.

Place the original box on the wrapping paper and follow steps 1 to 7 on pp. 12 and 13. Wrap aluminum foil around the wooden stick as shown, and punch the "antenna" into the top left of the package. Tape the perforated ribbon on the black glossy foil. Attach the glossy foil and 4 buttons with double-sided tape to the front of the "radio," and place 1 button to the right side and another on top.

Alarm Clock as Clutch Purse

"We bought this alarm clock for friends who value aesthetics and beautiful designs. They own a small furniture store and usually work late into the night. So, they rarely get out of bed on time mornings."

Material for an alarm clock:
Glossy wrapping paper 20 by 28 inches, 28 inches of reinforced metallic ribbon, double-sided tape.

1. Place the alarm clock on top of the glossy wrapping paper, and follow steps 2 to 6 on pp. 12 and 13. Tilt the alarm clock backward. Roll about four-fifths of the paper's back edge forward.

2. Attach double-sided tape to the left front of the roll, and tape one end of the reinforced metallic ribbon on it. Then wrap the other end of the ribbon along the package's underside to the right upper side of the roll.

3. Fold the end of the metallic ribbon into a triangular point. Tape the wrapping paper roll to the package, and then tape the metallic ribbon's triangular point on it.

BREAKABLE GIFTS

Plate as Angel

"Our company's management is presenting our co-worker a traditional silver anniversary plate to commemorate his 25th year with the firm. Our new boss would prefer to give him something different, but we cannot. So, let's at least wrap the plate imaginatively."

Material for a 10-inch plate:
Foil 40 inches square, foil 12 by 24 inches, cardboard roll (such as roll from paper towels), curling ribbon.

1. Place the plate in the middle of the large foil square, and set the cardboard roll in its middle.

2. Pull up all four corners of foil tightly over the roll, and tie them together with curling ribbon.

Then fold a bow tie out of the smaller foil, and tie it to the package with curling ribbon (see p. 20).

Plate Half Hidden

"My grandson is getting married, and I know that this silver plate will please him and his wife. So, I don't mind parting with this wonderful heirloom. I want them to recognize immediately what I've brought them for their wedding."

Material for a 10-inch plate:
Sturdy cardboard 16 inches square, glossy wrapping paper 20 by 34 inches, contrasting paper 20 by 28 inches, double-sided tape, sharp pencil.

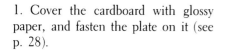

1. Cover the cardboard with glossy paper, and fasten the plate on it (see p. 28).

2. Lay the contrasting paper over four-fifths of the plate, and fold the front and back edges downward.

3. Then fold the paper's right side and the small left triangle of paper to the cardboard's underside. Tape the paper's edges to the back of the covered cardboard with double-sided tape.

Watch in Glass

"My youngest daughter is moving in with a friend. This is their first apartment. Everybody will be bringing a glass from a chosen set of stemware. But that seems too little as a housewarming gift. So we're also giving Sabine this wristwatch, which she has long fancied. I've already put it in the glass."

Since there's usually a lot needed in a young household, we put the glass into a box and tied it together with a dish towel, decorated with a ribbon rose. Certainly, everything will be useful.

Material:
Box, dish towel, curling ribbon, sharp pencil.
Rose:
40 inches of 4-inch ribbon.

With the pencil, punch two holes into the box's bottom, and tie the glass's stem to it with curling ribbon.

Close the box, wrap the dish towel around the box, and tie the towel together with curling ribbon. Fasten a ribbon rose to the towel (see pp. 14 and 15).

Paperweight in Crate of Apples

"The birthday kid, my office mate, collects paperweights," says the customer. He showed us a round glass paperweight with colorful ornaments inside. "I usually wrap presents myself, but this time I have no ideas."

When the customer mentioned that his office mate eats at least two apples a day, we chose a crate of apples as packaging.

Material:
Apple crate, tissue paper of assorted colors to wrap apples, paperweight.

Wrap the apples individually in the tissue paper, and place them in the crate. Also wrap the paperweight in a distinctive color and leave tissue paper full and loose on top (see photo). The office mate will certainly be surprised.

This packaging is suitable for all round gifts about the size of an apple.

Two Glasses on Leaf

"My sister especially likes two things—champagne and green plants. So, I bought her these glasses with flowers and leaves painted on them."

Material:
Philodendron or other large leaf, aspidistra leaves, smaller leaf, asparagus leaves, fresh 10-inch twig as thin as a pencil, 10-inch bast fibre or gold ribbon, 2 4-inch strands of 1¼-inch ribbon, soft work base.

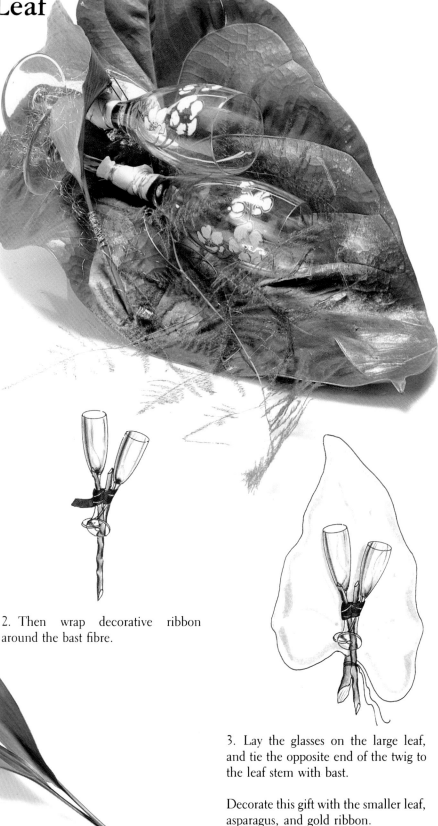

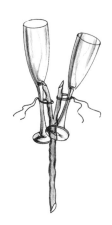

1. Lay the glasses on your work base. Split the twig so that it forks at one end about 6 inches long, and use bast fibre to tie one glass at the stem to each branch.

2. Then wrap decorative ribbon around the bast fibre.

3. Lay the glasses on the large leaf, and tie the opposite end of the twig to the leaf stem with bast.

Decorate this gift with the smaller leaf, asparagus, and gold ribbon.

70

Vase on Pedestal

"A friend of mine did me a big favor, so I want to thank him with this Chinese enamel vase. He has a special interest in the Far East."

Material:
2 square flat boxes of the same size, wrapping paper 8 by 12 inches and black on both sides, 20 inches of 4-inch ribbon, black curling ribbon. Ask someone to help you.

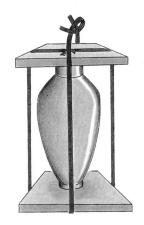

1. Place the vase on one of the boxes, using it as a pedestal. Put the other box on top of the vase. Now use curling ribbon to fasten this construction together (as shown). Tie the curling ribbon together tightly on top of the upper box. This will keep things from shifting out of place.

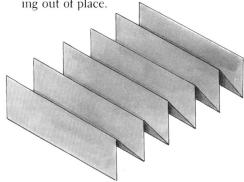

2. For the "fan," fold the wrapping paper into an accordion shape.

3. Slide the folded wrapping paper under the curling ribbon. Pull up the paper's ends to create a fan shape, and tape the top folds together on the inside with tape.

In front of the fan attach a bow created from the wide ribbon (see p. 18).

71

SYMBOLIC GIFTS

Money as Roof Luggage

"Susanne cannot wait until she finally owns her own car. We promised her money for her 18th birthday to help buy a car, but we don't want to give it to her in an unloving way. Here's the check that we want wrapped."

Material:
Model car, sturdy cardboard 8 by 14 inches, glossy wrapping paper 16 by 17 inches, silver foil 2¾ by 16 inches, small piece of glossy foil or paper, double-sided tape, curling ribbon, ribbon for small bow, sharp pencil.

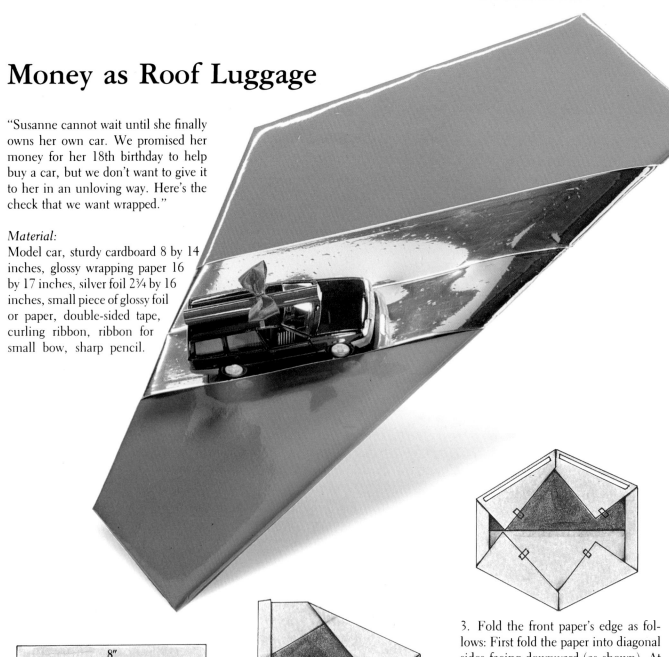

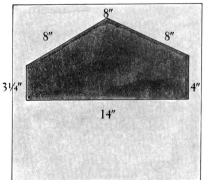

1. Cut the cardboard to the measurements shown in the drawing, and place it on the glossy wrapping paper.

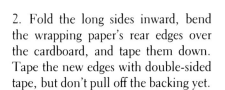

2. Fold the long sides inward, bend the wrapping paper's rear edges over the cardboard, and tape them down. Tape the new edges with double-sided tape, but don't pull off the backing yet.

3. Fold the front paper's edge as follows: First fold the paper into diagonal sides facing downward (as shown). At the folds created, fold the paper on the left and right inward and attach it to the double-sided tape. Tape the silver foil strip diagonally over the front surface. Tie on the car with curling ribbon (see p. 28).

Roll the bill or check into the glossy foil and fasten it to the car. If the car's windows can be opened, pull the curling ribbon through them, and tie the ribbon on the roll with a small glossy bow. Or tape the money onto the car as roof luggage.

74

Greeting Card with Bow

"Our trainee passed the exam, and we've collected money to help her out with her new career. She's a young romantic who is filled with fantasies."

Material:
Colored cardboard 20 by 14 inches and glossy on one side, 32 inches of 4-inch satin ribbon, 2 32-inch strips of 4-inch lace-and-satin ribbon, small envelope for money or check, double-sided tape.

1. Place the cardboard with the dull side facing upward. Attach the envelope with double-sided tape to the right side. Below people can sign their names. Across the left side of the cardboard lay a piece of lace ribbon.

2. Close the card, and tie the two ribbon ends together with yarn.

Fold the other lace ribbon to form a bow, and fasten it with yarn (see p. 18).

Concert Tickets in Sheet Music

People often give tickets and many different gift certificates as presents, but there are few unusual envelopes. But you can create your own without much effort in a variety of formats, patterns, and colors. We've used sheet music paper.

Material for an envelope 8 inches square:
Wrapping paper about 20 to 28 inches, double-sided tape.

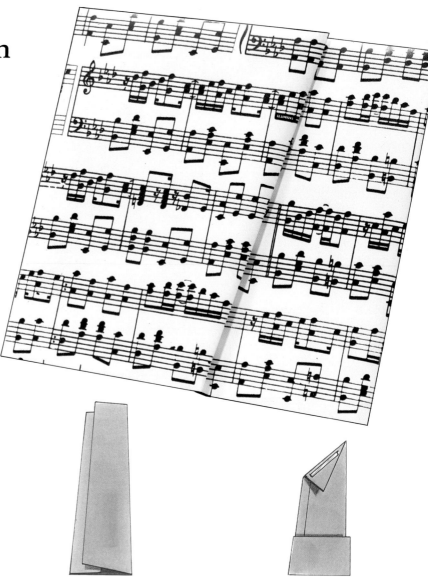

1. Fold the paper's left long sides 4 inches inward.

2. Bend the paper's right side over its left. The paper will now be 8 inches wide.

4. Fold the paper 8 inches back to create a pocket. Close the pocket on the sides with double-sided tape. Put the gift certificate or tickets inside.

    Fold in the paper's upper edge diagonally from left to right, and secure it with double-sided tape.

3. Fold the lower edge about 2 inches inward, and attach double-sided tape to the long sides.

5. Pull the paper forward and fasten it to the "pocket."

Gift Certificate in Recycled Envelope

"I've just heard that many communities ask consumers to avoid environmentally damaging gift wrappings and to look for alternatives. My family has collected money so that my sister can spend her vacation at the ocean. We want a unique wrapping for this vacation gift certificate. How could we combine uniqueness with something that won't hurt the environment?"

Material:
Sturdy cardboard 6¼ by 9¾ inches, corrugated cardboard 15¾ by 23½ inches, gift card, napkin, double-sided tape.

1. Place the gift certificate on the sturdy cardboard and then place both on the smooth side of the corrugated cardboard.

2. Fold the cardboard's front edge back; then pull the upper edge forward. The grooves of corrugated cardboard suggest waves.

3. Fold the napkin into a long strip, and lay it diagonally over the envelope and tape it to the envelope's underside.

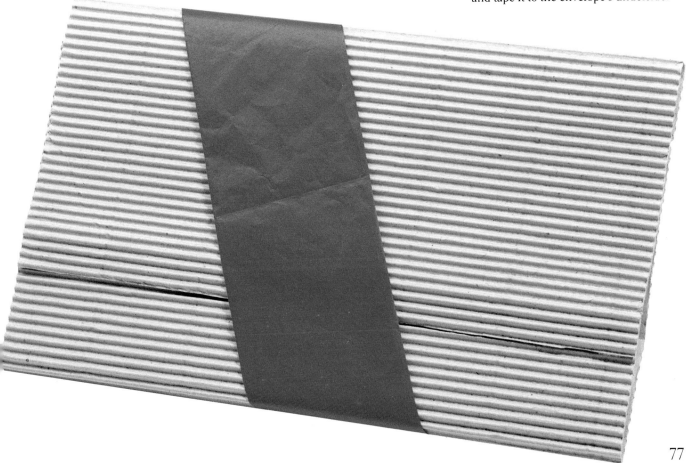

Invitation for Coffee

"Here's a present for my mother," the young man says. "I want to invite her for coffee on a regular basis. I know that she'd prefer that to my sending her flowers or other small gifts."

Material:
Sturdy cardboard 10 inches square, wrapping paper 20 by 28 inches and 14 by 28 inches, 2 pieces of 4-inch tulle—one 40 inches and one 60 inches long, mug, ground coffee, cookie, spoon, double-sided tape.

Cover the cardboard with the larger sheet of wrapping paper (see p. 28), and attach the mug to it with double-sided tape in the upper right quarter. Tie a "shoe bow" with the shorter tulle strip around the mug and a second bow with the longer piece of tulle around the cardboard's left side.

Fold the other wrapping paper into an envelope (see p. 76), and place your letter inside. Slide the envelope and spoon under the bow. Shortly before you present the gift, fill the mug with ground coffee, and stick the cookie halfway into it.

Letter to Say Good-bye

"We had a wonderful time together, but now we're going our separate ways. So that he knows I'll never forget him, I want this letter to be the nicest one he'll ever receive."

Material:
Sturdy cardboard 9 by 12 inches, glossy wrapping paper 16 by 20 inches and 14 by 15 inches, several pieces of tulle 4 inches square, double-sided tape, sharp pencil.

1. Cover the cardboard with the larger sheet of glossy wrapping paper (see p. 28), and lay the second sheet of wrapping paper on it diagonally, so that half of the letter can be slipped under it.

2. Fold the paper's left and right edges inward, but don't tape them on. Fold the upper edge that juts out and the small lower triangle to the back side of the cardboard. Fasten the paper edges with double-sided tape.

3. Punch 2 small holes into the upper left corner for the tulle.

79

INDEX

Metric Equivalents

INCHES TO MILLIMETRES AND CENTIMETRES

MM—millimetres   CM—centimetres

Inches	MM	CM	Inches	CM	Inches	CM
⅛	3	0.3	9	22.9	30	76.2
¼	6	0.6	10	25.4	31	78.7
⅜	10	1.0	11	27.9	32	81.3
½	13	1.3	12	30.5	33	83.8
⅝	16	1.6	13	33.0	34	86.4
¾	19	1.9	14	35.6	35	88.9
⅞	22	2.2	15	38.1	36	91.4
1	25	2.5	16	40.6	37	94.0
1¼	32	3.2	17	43.2	38	96.5
1½	38	3.8	18	45.7	39	99.1
1¾	44	4.4	19	48.3	40	101.6
2	51	5.1	20	50.8	41	104.1
2½	64	6.4	21	53.3	42	106.7
2	76	7.6	22	55.9	43	109.2
3½	89	8.9	23	58.4	44	111.8
4	102	10.2	24	61.0	45	114.3
4½	114	11.4	25	63.5	46	116.8
5	127	12.7	26	66.0	47	119.4
6	152	15.2	27	68.6	48	121.9
7	178	17.8	28	71.1	49	124.5
8	203	20.3	29	73.7	50	127.0